The Death of Public Knowledge?

Part of the Goldsmiths Press PERC series

Goldsmiths' Political Economy Research Centre (PERC) seeks to refresh political economy, in the original sense of the term, as a pluralist and critical approach to the study of capitalism. In doing so it challenges the sense of economics as a discipline, separate from the other social sciences, aiming instead to combine economic knowledge with various other disciplinary approaches. This is a response to recent critiques of orthodox economics, as immune to interdisciplinarity and cut off from historical and political events.

At the same time, the authority of economic experts and the relationship between academic research and the public (including, but not only, public policy-makers) are constant concerns running through PERC's work.

For more information please visit http://www.gold.ac.uk/perc/.

The Death of Public Knowledge?

How Free Markets Destroy
the General Intellect

Edited by Aeron Davis

Goldsmiths
Press

© 2017 Goldsmiths Press
Published in 2017 by Goldsmiths Press
Goldsmiths, University of London, New Cross
London SE14 6NW

Printed and bound in the United States of America.
Distribution by The MIT Press
Cambridge, Massachusetts, and London, England

A CIP record for this book is available from the British Library.

ISBN 978-1-906897-39-0 (hbk)
ISBN 978-1-906897-41-3 (ebk)

www.gold.ac.uk/goldsmiths-press

Goldsmiths
UNIVERSITY OF LONDON

Contents

Preface and Acknowledgements

This edited collection is the first book-length publication of Goldsmiths' new Political Economy Research Centre (PERC). PERC was launched in early 2015 alongside its new PPE (Philosophy, Politics and Economics) degree. It aims to promote research into and debate around alternatives to mainstream neoclassical economics. Its board and members range across heterodox economics, political economy, cultural economy, economic sociology and economic history. The main elements that unite PERC members are a sense of interdisciplinarity and an insistence that economics cannot be separated from social and political influences and events. Although based in academia, the centre also encourages exchanges with interest groups, think tanks and others across civil society.

This particular book comes out of the PERC Papers series. The items in this series began as short papers—crosses between a blog and an academic working paper—and all were first published online throughout 2015 and early 2016. They were to combine scholarly, informed writing with polemical commentary, applying this mix to contemporary events. Authors came from academia, journalism and campaigning organisations.

All pieces were especially commissioned under the theme of the economics of public knowledge. Each explores what is happening to types of public knowledge in its varied forms and settings, from mass media to public libraries and education, from financial markets to public policy-making in health care and defence. Each author observes a very real erosion of the kinds of information, media and public knowledge that are considered essential for polities, markets and societies to function properly. The most obvious causes appear to stem from the pervasive influence of neoliberal free market thinking, which inculcates competition into every area of social and political life.

However, declining public knowledge also has many other causes. The online world has destabilised the long-term business models by which journalism, publishing and many forms of popular culture operated. Public knowledge and culture are hard to evaluate and justify in an era in which audits and quantification are becoming the key mechanisms of modern political and market management. In a prolonged period of austerity and cuts, public knowledge in all its forms often suffers the first and deepest reductions. But in a time when knowledge is more specialist, fast-moving and complex, it is also short-lived. Knowledge redundancy is hard-wired into everything, from news to operating systems, from clothing fashions to investment fashions. Under such conditions, it is only large corporations and the very wealthy that can afford to keep paying for specialist knowledge—but they guard it fiercely for themselves. Thus, extremes of information inequality both reflect and contribute to those of material inequality.

In conclusion, I would like to thank all those who gave their time and own expert knowledge to writing a short piece for a fledgling centre and website. Thanks also to all who have lent much-needed institutional support to get PERC and PPE up and running in their early years, including Pat Loughrey and Roger Burrows, and to the core PERC management team of Will Davies, my co-director, Johnna Montgomerie and Zoe

Lake Thomas. Lastly, thanks to Sarah Kember, Michelle Lo and Adrian Driscoll at Goldsmiths Press, as well as the team at MIT Press for their work in taking on this project.

Aeron Davis
Co-Director of PERC

1

Introduction

Aeron Davis

This edited collection looks at the erosion of public knowledge in all its forms and explores the consequences of its decline. In the autumn of 2016, as this book goes into production, the issues addressed here look more pressing than ever: The United Kingdom appears to be a particularly divided and untrusting nation. It has recently voted to leave the European Union. Financial markets are unstable and seem ready to over-react to every new small piece of economic data. Both main parties appear thoroughly split, internally and externally; so too does much of the country, as EU 'leavers' and those who voted to remain ('remainers') look at each other with utter incredulity. A great sense of unease has descended: No one knows where Britain's long-established political, economic and social systems are headed.

Part of this sense of breakdown has emerged directly from the cynical and ill-informed public debates around Brexit. For many, the principal campaigners appeared to be arguing a case they hardly believed in. David Cameron, George Osborne and

Jeremy Corbyn, campaigning for Remain, had all shown moderate Eurosceptic beliefs in the past. Boris Johnson, for Leave, had previously sounded more pro-European and even advocated Turkey's entry into the EU (something presented as a threat by leavers).

Leave campaigners repeatedly lied about the economic gains and immigration cuts that would follow an EU exit. Economists, international leaders and institutions that argued to remain were dismissed as the kind of 'experts' that 'people have had enough of'. Analysis of news coverage of the referendum period revealed that the large majority of print news content was biased, and, if circulation figures are taken into account, 82 percent of such content promoted the Leave case (Loughborough University EU Referendum 2016).

The United Kingdom now seems to have moved into an Orwellian, post-truth era in which 'facts', leaders and rational arguments inspire little faith. However, as this book reveals, this era has long-term systemic roots—and it also is not restricted to the United Kingdom.

It was not so long ago that the UK and US governments spent billions to propagate the myth of Iraq's weapons of mass destruction (WMD). Since then, governments, not bankers, have somehow been held to blame for the financial crisis, with immigrants and the poor held to account for austerity and cuts. Such narratives are equally common across the US and EU nations (Picard 2014). This is also a time when stock markets, CEO salaries and property prices keep going up, all in spite of general economic stagnation. Inequality has been rising steadily everywhere since the 1980s (Piketty 2014), its pace quickening since the financial crash.

Populist leaders and post-truth politics are springing up everywhere. In the United States, Tea Party politics have produced gridlock in Washington. Donald Trump's success owes much to a similar breakdown of faith in the established political, media and economic systems of America. In addition, system upheavals threaten relatively wealthy and stable political economies, from France and Greece to Argentina and Brazil. Far right parties (e.g., Front National, Golden Dawn, Jobbik, DPP, UKIP) present serious challenges across Europe and are upending long-established parties and coalitions. Undoubtedly, in all these cases, substantial economic, political, social and environmental shifts are key factors. Clearly, the forty-year failed neoliberal experiment and the lack of post-financial-crisis alternatives have contributed.

However, this book argues that the long, slow death of public knowledge in all its forms is also a strong causal factor. The generation and dissemination of shared public knowledge is a foundational element of democracies, markets and societies everywhere. Without it, there is no social contract, no political legitimacy, no market transactions and no basis for common decision-making. There is also no sense of shared local or (inter)national identity or possibility of a more equal society.

Yet wherever austerity has bitten, competition has been propelled forward or individual choice proclaimed, it is public knowledge which has suffered first. Its erosion encourages more of the same and sets in motion a vicious circle of decline. Part of the problem is that the generation of public knowledge is very much an economic endeavour, influenced by political and economic institutions—as is the generation of economically relevant knowledge itself. Yet neither mainstream economics nor the political establishment shows much interest in something so taken for granted, unquantifiable and immaterial. Just as leaders everywhere continually focus on short-term gains at the expense of long-term investment, so the crisis of public knowledge mounts. Like global warming, inequality and economic instability, the collapse of public knowledge systems is threatening critical consequences.

The Perfect Storm Eroding Public Knowledge

Currently, public knowledge is under threat as never before; a perfect storm of factors is eroding it in all its forms. One of these factors is the Internet. On the one hand, the web offers an abundance of information on all manner of topics and from a wide range of sources. On the other, it has undermined the business models on which public knowledge and cultural creation have relied. Advertising has steadily migrated away from traditional media. Copyright of content is impossible to enforce, which in turn deters investment in its creation. The rise of new digital distributors with global power has weakened the hands of many content producers (McChesney 2014).

A second factor is everything that follows from the long march towards neoliberalism in the organisation of our society. Making public knowledge and culture a matter of individual choice means that the 'general intellect' is not treated as a social or national resource. State-funded knowledge and entertainment increasingly gives way to market-funded formats with no incentive to support worthy but unprofitable outputs.

Third is budget cuts and austerity economics. For mainstream economists and right-wing parties, public knowledge is no different from any other public provision and consequently should be produced by markets rather than states. For political economists and left-wing parties, it is more important to protect the material than the cultural. Real food is more essential than food for the mind.

Fourth is the nature of modern knowledge itself. It is increasingly complex, technical, fast-moving and over-loaded. That puts it beyond the comprehension of most people, including those at the centre of decision-making processes. This also leads to greater reliance on so-called experts and technicians with specialist but narrow world views—a world of disconnected information silos that few may access (Engelen et al. 2011).

Fifth is the rise of inequality, concentrated corporate power and the super-rich (Piketty 2014). Extreme inequalities allow the 1 percent to buy the best forms of specialist knowledge, which were once more equally distributed, in accounting and taxation, in law, in economic and financial market research, in public affairs and in advanced communication technologies. Public institutions cannot match the knowledge-producing and purchasing facilities of big finance and business, let alone offer them to wider publics. Thus the decline of public knowledge and knowledge inequalities are directly related to inequality more generally.

Sixth is the rise of forms of 'econocracy' (Davis, forthcoming) and 'auditocracy' (or *audit society*; Power 1997): the rise to the top of economically oriented leaders in the fields of politics, public administration and business. Across Westminster, Whitehall and business associations, general knowledge and experience are giving way to economic knowledge, accountancy and targets. In many ways, forms of public knowledge production do not fit. Outputs of news, culture and specialist research can be easily quantified, but not so the resources involved in their production. The emphasis on increasing quantified outputs inevitably erodes the quality and degree of depth in their inputs.

The Erosion of Public Knowledge Provision: A Business Model in Decline

Most obviously, the erosion of public knowledge is observable in the decline and privatisation of the institutions and organisations that traditionally generate and circulate it. In the immediate aftermath of the 2010 UK general election, higher education was the first institution subjected to radical marketisation as fees tripled to £9,000 and the government attempted (but has failed so far) to securitize the student loan book (McGettigan 2013). Local library capacity has been cut back significantly as local authorities have been forced to endure drastic cuts. Combined library expenditure has fallen by a third since 2005/2006. Expenditure on books and digital content is the lowest it has been for twenty years (Public Libraries News 2014).

Mainstream news providers in the United Kingdom, United States and elsewhere have watched audiences and advertising revenues slowly decline over several decades. However, the pace of decline has quickened considerably in the twenty-first century with the rise of online news outlets, news aggregators and digital entertainment. Pew Research Center (2012) calculates that the US newspaper industry shrunk 43 percent and lost 28 percent of journalist jobs between 2000 and 2012. In that time, on average, fifteen papers entered bankruptcy each year. In 2011, US newspapers gained $207 million in online advertising but lost $2.1 billion in print advertising. The *Guardian*, which led the UK press sector in developing its online presence, had gained sixty million unique users by December 2011, but at the same time saw its pre-tax losses rise to £171 million for the year (Franklin 2012). Many areas of news—including local, investigative, parliamentary and foreign reporting—have been particularly hard hit.

In all these areas, institutions and organisations have been forced to adapt to survive, often reducing their product to something that only weakly resembles the services and contents they once produced. One survival strategy is to increase outputs per employee: bigger classes per teacher or academic tutor, more articles or broadcasts per journalist. In his 2008 book, Davies estimated that UK journalists had to fill three times as much news space as they did in the 1980s (Davies 2008). Another strategy involves the de-professionalisation of knowledge-producing sectors and the harnessing of cheap or voluntary labour. Thus, universities have increasingly come to rely on temporary visiting tutors to teach growing numbers of students. Since 2007, two-fifths of professionally qualified library staff have been cut, whereas voluntary staff have increased 2.5-fold (Public Libraries News 2014). Meanwhile, news media has become more dependent on the contributions of freelancers, temporary staff, amateur citizen journalists and user-generated content. So too does television production look to reality TV shows and competitions, made with low-cost participants, as a cheap alternative to higher-cost documentaries and dramas.

Most concerning of all is the third strategy of public knowledge producers: to become reliant on funding and 'information subsidies' from the very sources they are supposed to report on. Academic and regulatory research institutions are pushed to seek out business funds and sponsors, which then have a say on published outputs (Monbiot 2000). Most news reporting outlets (public broadcasters excepted) have always been reliant on commercial advertising to heavily subsidise content, thus leaving difficult professional conflicts of interest for journalists (Curran and Seaton 2009). However, as news organisations struggle they have become increasingly dependent on a range of additional information subsidies: news wire services, recycled material, plagiarised copy from rival publications and, above all, public relations outputs from commercial and political sources.

In the United States, according to McChesney and Nichols in their 2010 book, there were four times as many public relations practitioners as media editorial staff working in 2008. An estimated 40 to 50 percent of newspaper stories began life as press releases, while only 14 percent originated from reporters. Lewis, Williams and Franklin's 2008 study of UK news found that 19 percent of press stories and 17 percent of broadcasts were entirely or mainly reproduced PR material. Forty-nine percent of press stories were either entirely or mainly dependent on news wire agency copy. Thus, be it reporting of foreign conflicts (Herman and Chomsky 2002), scientific research and big pharma (Goldacre 2013) or climate change (Klein 2014), public news and information is far from autonomous and objective.

The Free Market Corruption of Public Knowledge in Markets

The breakdown of the economic model of public knowledge and culture has been matched by a similar decline in the creation of specialist, economically relevant information used by markets, regulators and policy-makers. 'Big Bang' in the UK in 1985–1986 was intended to create real competition and more efficient trading in the London Stock Exchange, but instead it created a system whereby international investment banks ended up providing information and advice to both buyers and sellers as well as their own investment arms (Augar 2000). Market forces encouraged low-cost trading and multiple participants, but at the same time devalued and corrupted the production and dissemination of investment research and market-relevant information. Financial journalists and analysts alike became dependent on self-interested investor relations material produced by sellers and the self-serving analyses of investment banks (Davis 2007). The degradation of financial market information in the city was a strong contributory factor to the dotcom boom of the 1990s and the bust that followed in 2000. In effect, the application of extreme market forces to markets themselves has resulted in the corruption of market-relevant information within those markets.

A similar story has unfolded with financial markets in the United States and with a series of financial scandals, bubbles and crises in many nations (Lewis 2011, 2014; Engelen et al. 2011; Ferguson 2012). The sub-prime mortgage bubble, the massive rise of derivatives markets, the general expansion of the shadow banking sector, the growth of high-frequency trading and the Libor scandal all have much in common. They all involve abundant flows of low-cost lending, insiders and outsiders, and conflicts of interest. However, they also share problems associated with the production, dissemination and regulation of market information. New communication technologies, deregulation and the complexity of modern finance each have contributed to massive information inequalities and information corruption across markets. Not only are outsiders continually disadvantaged, regulators and credit-rating agencies cannot keep up. They are unable to access what is happening in the shadow banking sector, in the OTC derivatives market and in the 'dark pool' trading centres of finance. Neither are they able to effectively rate the risks of new financial products nor spot cumulative, market-wide risks building up.

The Corruption of Public Knowledge Used to Inform Economic Policy, Regulation and Taxation

A comparable set of problems are present when it comes to accounting, taxation and economic policy. Four big accountancy firms dominate when it comes to both auditing companies and offering these same organisations accounting services. The same big four advise governments and tax inspectors on accountancy regulations. It is the same investment bank managers who get senior positions in government treasuries and regulatory institutions before returning to those same investment banks, and the same esteemed economists write authoritative reports used in decision-making that are paid for by vested interests (Ferguson 2012; Shaxson 2012; Murphy 2013). In effect, the production of financial and economic information that is used to inform decision-making on behalf of the public is itself riddled with conflicts of interest. This allows tax avoidance by big business and the super-rich on a massive scale. It also produces regressive taxation systems that facilitate the continuing transfer of capital from the poorest to the richest 1 percent.

If accountancy and taxation public knowledge is compromised, so is public knowledge in other areas that inform public policy and regulation of the economy. Rich and powerful individuals and organisations have always had more privileged access to political and administrative decision-makers (Lukes 2005), but they are now advantaged more than ever because of their influence over the creation of specialist economic and market knowledge that becomes used by non-expert politicians and civil servants. As economics, finance and science have become more fast-moving and complex, we have entered the age of technical experts and specialist information intermediaries. These include lawyers, lobbyists, think tankers and financiers as well as economists and accountants (Cave and Rowell 2014). It is the super-rich and large corporations that can now afford to pay for the brightest and most able in these professions and to buy as much expertise and research as is necessary.

Thus it is financiers themselves and their many information intermediaries who have had most input into how the financial sector is regulated since 2007/2008. In the United States, lobbying expenditure from the securities and investment sectors amounted to $932 million between 1998 and 2012. From the insurance sector, it was $1.7 billion (OpenSecrets 2012). In the United Kingdom, the Bureau of Investigative Journalism (2012) found that the UK financial sector spent an estimated £92.8 million lobbying the UK government. The Bureau identified 129 organisations engaged in lobbying for finance. Firms of accountants, lobbyists, PR experts and financiers also directly fund or offer pro bono expertise to all the main parties and their think tanks. In recent years, the financial sector has provided over 50 percent of the Conservative Party's funds (Peston 2011). In effect, once again it is the rich and powerful funding or creating public policy information on economic and financial matters. Public policy-making research and analysis has been contracted out to organisations for which the main pursuit is self-interest rather than public interest (Crouch 2004). Consequently, rational public decision-making on economic and financial matters, based on 'independent expert research', results in tainted and partial outcomes regardless of the party in power.

In conclusion, any progressive form of politics and economics—that is, one that values equality and a notion of a shared society—must acknowledge the importance of public knowledge. Public knowledge and culture, in all its forms, must be seen as a fundamental right, not an additional luxury, and be supported accordingly. Its valuation must resist the tendency to a crude reductionism based on numbers and competition logics. Content creation and authorship needs to be more rigorously upheld by law. The generation of specialist knowledge and public policy needs to be funded by the public purse rather than vested interests. Legal, political and market institutions must operate independently of market forces and partial 'information subsidies' when it comes to generating and disseminating wider public information.

References

Augar, P. 2000. *The Death of Gentlemanly Capitalism*. London: Penguin.

Bureau of Investigative Journalism. 2012. July. http://www.thebureau investigates.com.

Cave, T., and A. Rowell. 2014. *A Quiet Word: Crony Capitalism and Broken Politics in Britain*. London: Bodley Head.

Crouch, C. 2004. *Post Democracy*. Cambridge: Polity.

Curran, J., and J. Seaton. 2009. *Power without Responsibility: Press, Broadcasting and the Internet in Britain*. London: Routledge.

Davies, N. 2008. *Flat Earth News*. London: Chatto and Windus.

Davis, A. 2007. *The Mediation of Power: A Critical Introduction*. London: Routledge.

Davis, A. Forthcoming. "The New Professional Econocracy and the Maintenance of Elite Power." *Political Studies*.

Engelen, E., I. Erturk, J. Froud, S. Johal, A. Leaver, M. Moran, A. Nilsson, and K. Williams. 2011. *After the Great Complacence: Financial Crisis and the Politics of Reform*. Oxford: Oxford University Press.

Ferguson, C. 2012. *Inside Job: The Financiers Who Pulled Off the Heist of the Century*. Oxford: Oneworld.

Franklin, B. 2012. "The Future of Journalism: Developments and Debates." *Journalism Studies* 13 (5-6): 663-681.

Goldacre, B. 2013. *Bad Pharma: How Medicine Is Broken and How We Can Fix It*. London: Fourth Estate.

Herman, E., and N. Chomsky. 2002. *Manufacturing Consent: The Political Economy of the Mass Media*. 2nd ed. New York: Pantheon Books.

Klein, N. 2014. *This Changes Everything: Capitalism versus the Climate*. London: Allen Lane.

Lewis, J., A. Williams, and B. Franklin. 2008. "A Compromised Fourth Estate? UK News Journalism, Public Relations and News Sources." *Journalism Studies* 9 (1): 1-20.

Lewis, M. 2011. *The Big Short: Inside the Doomsday Machine*. London: Penguin.

Lewis, M. 2014. *Flashboys*. London: Allen Lane.

Loughborough University EU Referendum. 2016. http://www.lboro.ac.uk/news-events/eu-referendum/.

Lukes, S. 2005. *Power: A Radical View*. Houndsmill, Basingstoke, UK: Palgrave Macmillan.

McChesney, R., and J. Nichols. 2010. *The Death and Life of American Journalism*. New York: Nation Books.

McChesney, R. 2014. *Digital Disconnect: How Capitalism Is Turning the Internet against Democracy*. New York: The New Press.

McGettigan, A. 2013. *The Great University Gamble: Money, Markets and the Future of Higher Education*. London: Pluto Press.

Monbiot, G. 2000. *Captive State: The Corporate Takeover of Britain*. Basingstoke: Pan Books.

Murphy, R. 2013. *Over Here and Undertaxed: Multinationals, Tax Avoidance and You*. London: Vintage Digital.

OpenSecrets. 2012. http://www.opensecrets.org/index.php.

Peston, R. 2011. "More than Half of Conservative Donors from the City. BBC News. September 11. http://www.bbc.co.uk/news/uk-politics-12401049.

Pew Research Center. 2012. *The State of the News Media Reports*. Washington, DC: Pew/The Project for Excellence in Journalism.

Picard, R., ed. 2014. *The Euro Crisis in the Media*. London: I. B. Taurus.

Piketty, T. 2014. *Capital in the Twenty-First Century*. Cambridge, MA: Harvard University Press.

Power, M. 1997. *The Audit Society: Rituals of Verification*. Oxford: Oxford University Press.

Public Libraries News. 2014. http://www.publiclibrariesnews.com.

Shaxson, N. 2012. *Treasure Islands: Tax Havens and the Men Who Stole the World*. London: Vintage.

I

Public News Media

The future of public service media is of special concern in the United Kingdom, where, following the 2015 election, the Conservatives have made a series of cuts to the BBC and set in motion reviews about its future funding and governance. Likewise, the future status of Channel Four, the United Kingdom's commercially funded public service broadcaster, is also being reconsidered. The threat to the public service remits of both organisations is a particular worry when the large majority of print media are owned by Conservative-supporting owners. However, as the chapters in part I will reveal, public service media is now struggling to survive in many nations, and several offer insights into what a future British media landscape might look like.

In chapter 2, Toril Aalberg compares public and private media systems across a range of nations. Aalberg, who has worked on a number of international, comparative projects, finds that public service media do more than commercial outlets to inform citizens in democracies. Sifting through the conclusions of multiple studies, she finds that public service media systems offer more depth and hard news coverage on balance, and consequently their citizens are more informed about current affairs.

Next, Aristotelis Nikolaidis (chapter 3) investigates what has happened to Greek public media since the financial crisis hit and harsh austerity measures were imposed on the country. As he explains, Greek private media was already overly linked with big business before the crisis. Since the crisis, public news media have been significantly cut back, leaving private media in a dominant position to set reporting agendas and frames. In consequence, mainstream media coverage heavily favours corporate interests and right-wing politics. Thus such coverage has continued to argue for austerity measures and strongly supported acceptance of recent EU bailout agreements.

In chapter 4, Wayne Hope recounts the recent history of news and current affairs media in New Zealand. The lurch towards neoliberalism was quicker in New Zealand in the 1980s, as what was then the Labour Government embraced market reforms with greater zeal than the United States or the United Kingdom. As this chapter explains, the consequence is that a thriving public media has been decimated, leaving foreign multinationals—often investment banks and private equity firms— largely in control. Thus, the New Zealand experience offers a stark warning about how neoliberal communication policies can lead to a financialized public sphere.

The BBC is generally seen as a publicly funded broadcaster, independent of advertising and kept fairly autonomous from government. However, as Kate Wright shows in chapter 5, large, post-2010 cuts have encouraged the BBC to seek additional advertising from its international-facing online component. Over a relatively short period, this has meant changes to editorial parameters and to the way the BBC presents itself. For example, consider how popular features are currently displacing hard news on the home screen. Wright's chapter demonstrates the nature of the shift through her study of NGO coverage in Africa.

In chapter 6, Rodney Benson concludes part I with a look at the evolving, digitalised news media environment in the hyper-commercialised US system. Here, the combination of the Internet, under-supported public media and financial crises has hit traditional news operations hard but failed to spawn a set of independent, financially viable online alternatives. The choice is stark: either elite news subscriptions or entirely commercialised news operations in which Pulitzer prizes mean lower share prices.

2

Does Public Media Enhance Citizen Knowledge? Sifting through the Evidence

Toril Aalberg

Political information is to democratic politics what money is to economics: it is the currency of citizenship.
—Delli Carpini and Keeter, *What Americans Know about Politics and Why It Matters*

Although there are disagreements about how politically knowledgeable citizens should be for democracy to function well, few argue against the notion that an informed citizenry is good for democracy. Because most citizens get their information about politics and current affairs from the media, a key concern for political communication scholars has been investigating the links between (1) media funding and organization and (2) the supply of political information and public knowledge.

To understand these mechanisms is perhaps more important now than ever before, as the media landscape is radically expanding and the number of commercial media channels multiplying. The challenge to existing media brought by this expansion is assumed to be a positive development, as citizen choices are enhanced. Such positive expectations about the emerging commercial media are mirrored by a rise in the number of questions about the relevance of publicly funded journalism. In many countries, there is now a heated debate about whether public media is distortive and stifles growth, innovation and plurality in the sector. However, as argued here, more commercial media does not automatically mean a more informed public. In fact, paradoxically, a higher number of information providers may result in a less informed democracy.

The purpose of this text is not to review these national political disputes. Instead, its aim is to provide a short and accessible assessment of current research on the supply and quality of hard news reporting in public and more commercially driven news media and to discuss how these media may influence political knowledge and public awareness.

Public versus Commercial Media in the Supply of News and Current Affairs

Recent comparative studies have shown that the status of public service media and their market impact vary considerably between nations (Hallin and Mancini 2004; Benson and Powers 2011; Rövekamp 2014). In some countries, the media system is highly fragmented and mostly commercial, like the American and Australian media sectors. In most other Western democratic states, however, there is a more balanced mix of public and private media. In many cases, public broadcasters are also the dominant media outlet, both in terms of audience size and in terms of quality and independence. In Western and Northern regions of Europe, public service broadcasters have received large amounts of governmental support. In contrast, audiences for public service channels in Australia, the United States, Canada and many countries in Eastern and Southern Europe tend to be significantly smaller.

Many public service broadcasters have experienced a severe funding crisis in recent years, as politicians and publics have become more skeptical about the role public media can (and should) play in the future. To remain relevant in a twenty-first-century media landscape, public service *broadcasters* have begun supplying online and social media platforms and, in the process, become known as public service *media* (Donders, Pauwels, and Loisen 2012). Nevertheless, they have continued to operate under a remit that promotes the 'public good' and serves the needs of all citizens (Cushion 2012; Hendy 2012). Typically, it is thus argued that public media should be distinctive from commercial competitors and pursue normative values, such as producing appealing content for all citizens—including minority groups—and pursuing an editorially diverse and independent agenda (Tracey 1998). Public media are also justified on the basis of their ability to better inform citizens as commercial media chase audiences and advertisers to survive. It is argued that market incentives will therefore lead to an overproduction of content that is popular, to the detriment of that which informs and empowers citizens about public affairs. Side-stepping entrenched political positions, what does the empirical research contribute to this debate?

The research evidence is somewhat mixed, but a majority of studies tend to support the assessment that there are significant differences between public and private media content. For instance, the general conclusions from schedule analyses, presented by Aalberg, van Aelst and Curran (2010) and Esser et al. (2012) show that public service media offer better political information opportunities than commercial media. When comparing the top two public service and commercial broadcasters in each country during periods when many media markets were deregulated and commercialised, a common finding was that market-driven channels gradually enhanced the availability of news. This challenged the belief that commercialization has diminished the supply of news altogether.

However, both studies also stressed that the presence of public service broadcasting within a national media ecology appeared to ensure that news continued to be scheduled at peak time. In other words, in 'countries where public television has a stronger standing, the public are offered more prime-time news and current affairs, not only by PBS channels but also by commercial ones' (Aalberg, van Aelst, and Curran 2010, 266). In contrast, in the market-driven media environment of the United States, there was a distinct lack of news programming and current affairs, including less at peak times and less on the most popular channels. These studies also demonstrate that established public service channels generally deliver more news than their commercial counterparts. This finding is supported by van Santen and Vliengenhart's 2013 study of Dutch TV programming over a fifty-year period. This study recorded that commercial broadcasters spent less time on information and more time on 'infotainment' and entertainment than Dutch public service channels.

An important limitation to studying broadcasting schedules, however, is that they cannot provide evidence about the quality of information provided. Accordingly, Esser et al. (2012) speculate about whether or not the positive effect of the growing amount of information is at least partly wiped out by rising levels of soft news with less relevance to the democratic process. One approach to evaluate the quality of news is to distinguish between 'hard' and 'soft' news, or pure information and infotainment. Reinemann et al. (2012, 234) define *hard news* as media content that is politically relevant for society as a whole and based on impersonal and unemotional reporting. *Soft news*, on the other hand, is viewed as less political and more focused on individuals and thus on personal and emotional reporting.

Research evidence about longitudinal changes in the supply of hard versus soft news is mixed (Reinemann et al. 2012). Although some studies suggest that news has not become 'softer' over recent decades (Scott and Gobetz 1992; Waldahl, Andersen, and Rønning 2009), others have found evidence to suggest the opposite (Patterson 2000; Donsbach and Büttner 2005; Sinardet, De Swert, and Dandoy 2004). It is also important to note that public service broadcasters with large audiences do not automatically foster hard news environments. For instance, although widely watched, the Italian public service broadcaster does not seem to generate a lot of hard news (Aalberg et al. 2013; Reinemann, Stanyer, and Scherr 2016).

However, several recent studies have identified clear differences in terms of hard and soft news content in public service and commercial media. For example, Maier, Ruhrmann and Stengel's 2009 study of seven different German television newscasts between 1992 and 2007 found significant differences. Although there is a linear increase of non-political content in commercial channels, this is not the case in newscasts provided by the public service channels. Aalberg et al. (2013) found that public service providers across nine different countries supplied more hard news on foreign affairs than commercial broadcasters, who pursued more of an international soft news agenda. As it is costly to assemble hard, thematic news, especially in foreign countries, the authors suggest that this may be a response to corporate commercial considerations. Reinemann, Stanyer and Scherr's 2016 comprehensive study of sixteen Western democracies demonstrated that public service broadcasters in general provided more hard news than commercial television networks, even after controlling for how commercialised the media system was.

Hence, one of the main conclusions of much of this literature is that the 'ecological effects' of strong public service television center on its contribution to a general climate in which media are more likely to report about politics in more substantial ways.

Media Systems and Public Knowledge

Publicly supported media systems tend to provide greater opportunities for citizens to encounter informative news, and many comparative studies therefore argue that citizens also are more likely to learn from it (Aalberg and Curran 2012; Curran et al. 2009; Iyengar et al. 2010; Soroka et al. 2013). Put simply, countries that support and help fund public journalism and that therefore offer a larger share of substantive news content to large audiences produce a better learning environment than those with market-driven media systems, through which quality news is less easily available.

These favorable opportunity structures are determined not only by the sheer volume of news and information, but also by their extensive distribution to a large and heterogenic audience. For instance, the placement of news and current affairs between popular shows and in attractive timeslots is seen to engage 'inadvertent' audiences—that is, those viewers who had not planned to watch the news but came across it accidently. Blumler (1970) first recognised the democratic value of reaching such audiences through these smart 'traps'.

Several recent empirical studies have supported this thesis (Curran et al. 2009; Iyengar et al. 2010), with reference to the public service versus commercial media debate. Aalberg and Curran (2012) demonstrate, for instance, that the knowledge gap between the interested and the uninterested is relatively small in many European countries, but this gap is quite dramatic in the United States. Citizens who were very interested in politics and who declared that they follow domestic politics closely were indeed very well informed across all countries and media systems, including the commercial US system. However, although uninterested citizens in Europe still managed to be relatively well informed, this was not the case in the United States, where a substantial minority had minimal news media exposure and remained politically uninformed. Insights from these studies suggest that the larger and increased knowledge gap in the more market-oriented US media system indicates that learning about politics is a more *active* process than in many European countries. US citizens are now required to work harder to actively seek out the news (Prior 2007).

The more extensive information environments offered by media systems with stronger public service providers, by contrast, stimulate more *passive learning*. Shehata's 2013 study, using Swedish panel data, found that exposure to news at election time had stronger effects on current affairs learning among citizens with lower levels of general political knowledge. This occurred despite the fact that these news programs are watched less extensively by this group of citizens, simply because they learn more from news exposure than high-information groups. Shehata thus concluded that 'the smaller current affairs knowledge gaps found in public service-oriented countries are, at least partly, the result of passive learning from television's inadvertent audiences who are captured by the extensive political information opportunities provided by the major television channels' (2013, 217). However, the new tendency toward watching television content online, rather than live, may reduce this inadvertent audience effect (Prior 2007).

Shehata (2013) did not control for the different effects of exposure to public service versus commercial media. However, as in other studies, his data suggested that the most knowledgeable citizens tended to prefer public service channels, whereas the less informed, to a larger extent, watch commercial news. Strömbäck's Swedish study (2015), however, did find that exposure to public service news lead to positive knowledge effects, whereas exposure to commercial news had negative knowledge effects. These results hold even after stringent controls, including general prior political knowledge.

An important innovation in media effects research is to control for self-selection tendencies within particular audiences (Soroka et al. 2013; Fraile and Iyengar 2014). Soroka and his colleagues (2013) found that compared to commercial news, public service broadcasters had a positive influence on news knowledge. However, not all public service providers were equally effective in this way (e.g., the effect of exposure to the Italian public broadcaster was actually negative). In the United Kingdom, there was a clear positive effect of exposure to news from public service broadcasters and a clear negative effect of exposure to commercial news. Also controlling for self-selection of news, Fraile and Iyengar (2014) found that public broadcasters had more informative effects than commercial broadcasters on unmotivated citizens, but exposure to broadsheet newspapers generally overshadow the positive effect of public service news exposure.

The empirical evidence also suggests that differences in national news supply influence not only how much citizens know about politics, but also the type of knowledge learnt. One of the patterns found in many studies is that Americans are less informed about international news compared to people in less market-driven media systems (e.g., Aalberg et al. 2013). Another, perhaps more important type of current affairs knowledge is marked by citizens' ability to describe issue positions of main political parties. A surprisingly large number of citizens find it impossible to do this, however (Jenssen, Aalberg, and Aarts 2012, 144). Among citizens with low hard current affairs knowledge, more than half of the respondents were unable to describe parties' issue positions. Jenssen, Aalberg and Aarts (2012) investigated whether the media was able to help lift people out of this political ignorance. They found that exposure to public service news had the most positive effect, whereas exposure to news from commercial broadcasters was less important. Similarly, Banducci, Giebler and Kritzinger (2015), using the European Election Study from 2009, showed that citizens who obtain information via quality news outlets (including public service broadcasters) had a better understanding of parties' policy positions than voters who received their information through low-quality outlets (including commercial broadcasters).

Conclusion

This chapter suggests that citizens are more likely to be exposed to hard news and be more knowledgeable about current affairs if they watch public service news or news in public service–dominated media systems, compared to more market-driven news environments. Although there is some mixed evidence, the overall picture indicates that media economy and public knowledge are related. The quality of the information environment and the positive effect of public service providers are based on institutional independence. Commercial broadcasters clearly provide citizens with more news opportunities if they need to comply with certain regulations and compete with a relatively strong public broadcaster. Despite the amount of news steadily increasing over recent decades, with more commercial choice and competition, this review suggests that public service media remain distinctly different from market-driven news and that they clearly are more effective in engendering informed citizenship.

References

Aalberg, T., and J. Curran. 2012. *How Media Inform Democracy: A Comparative Approach*. London: Routledge.

Aalberg, T., S. Papathanassopoulos, S. Soroka, J. Curran, K. Hayashi, S. Iyengar, P. Jones, G. Mazzolini, H. Rojas, D. Rowe, and R. Tiffen. 2013. "International TV News, Foreign Affairs Interest and Public Knowledge: A Comparative Study of Foreign News Coverage and Public Opinion in 11 Countries." *Journalism Studies* 14 (3): 387–406.

Aalberg, T., P. van Aelst, and J. Curran. 2010. "Media System and the Political Information Environment: A Cross-National Comparison." *International Journal of Press/Politics* 15 (3): 255–271.

Banducci, S., H. Giebler, and S. Kritzinger. 2015. "Knowing More from Less: How the Information Environment Increases Knowledge of Party Positions." *British Journal of Political Science*, August 24. https://www.cambridge.org/core/services/aop-cambridge-core/content/view/96D683F52DC8B3685717D EAF9C2D3FE5/S0007123415000204a.pdf/div-class-title-knowing-more-from -less-how-the-information-environment-increases-knowledge-of-party -positions-div.pdf.

Benson, R., and M. Powers. 2011. *Public Media and Political Independence: Lessons for the Future of Journalism from around the World*. New York: Free Press.

Blumler, J. G. 1970. "The Political Effects of Television." In *The Political Effects of Television*, edited by James D. Halloran, 68–104. London: Panther.

Curran, J., S. Iyengar, A. B. Lund, and I. Salovaara-Moring. 2009. "Media System, Public Knowledge and Democracy: A Comparative Study." *European Journal of Communication* 24 (1): 5–26.

Cushion, S.. 2012. *The Democratic Value of News: Why Public Service Media Matter*. Basingstoke, UK: Palgrave Macmillan.

Delli Carpini, M., and S. Keeter. 1996. *What Americans Know about Politics and Why It Matters*. New Haven, CT: Yale University Press.

Donders, K., C. Pauwels, and J. Loisen. 2012. "Introduction: All or Nothing? From Public Service Broadcasting to Public Service Media, to Public Service 'Anything'?" *International Journal of Media and Cultural Politics* 8 (1): 3–12.

Donsbach, W., and K. Büttner. 2005. "Boulevardisierungstrend in deutschen Fernsehnachrichten." *Publizistik* 50 (1): 21–38.

Esser, F., C. H. de Vreese, J. Strömbäck, P. van Aelst, T. Aalberg, J. Stanyer, G. Lengauer, R. Berganza, G. Legnante, S. Papathanassopoulos, S. Salgado, T. Sheafer, and C. Reinemann. 2012. "Political Information Opportunities in Europe: A Longitudinal and Comparative Study of Thirteen Television Systems." *International Journal of Press/Politics* 17 (3): 247–274.

Fraile, M., and S. Iyengar. 2014. "Not All News Sources Are Equally Informative: A Cross-National Analysis of Political Knowledge in Europe." *International Journal of Press/Politics* 19 (3): 275–294.

Hallin, D. C., and P. Mancini. 2004. *Comparing Media Systems: Three Models of Media and Politics*. Cambridge: Cambridge University Press.

Hendy, D. 2012. *Public Service Broadcasting.* Basingstoke, UK: Palgrave.

Iyengar, S., J. Curran, A. B. Lund, Inka Salovaara-Moring, K. S. Hahn, and S. Coen. 2010. "Cross-National versus Individual-Level Differences in Political Information: A Media Systems Perspective." *Journal of Elections, Public Opinion, and Parties* 20 (3): 291–309.

Jenssen, A. T., T. Aalberg, and K. Aarts. 2012. "Informed Citizens, Media Use and Public Knowledge of Parties Policy Positions." In *How Media Inform Democracy: A Comparative Approach*, edited by Toril Aalberg and James Curran, 138–158. New York: Routledge.

Maier, M., G.g Ruhrmann, and K. Stengel. 2009. *Der Wert von Nachrichten im deutschen Fernsehen: Inhaltsanalyse von TV-Nachrichten im Jahr 2007* [News values in German TV: A content analysis of TV news in 2007]. Düsseldorf: Landesanstalt für Medien.

Patterson, T. E. 2000. *Doing Well and Doing Good: How Soft News Are Shrinking the News Audience and Weakening Democracy.* Cambridge, MA: Harvard University Press.

Prior, M. 2007. *Post-broadcast Democracy: How Media Choice Increases Inequality in Political Involvement and Polarizes Elections.* New York: Cambridge University Press.

Reinemann, C., J. Stanyer, G. Legnante, and S. Scherr. 2012. "Hard News and Soft News: A Review of Concepts, Operationalizations and Key Findings." *Journalism: Theory, Practice and Criticism* 13 (2): 221–239.

Reinemann, C., J. Stanyer, and S. Scherr. 2016. "Hard and Soft News." In *Where's the Good News? Comparing Political Online and Offline Journalism in 16 Countries*, edited by Claes de Vreese, Frank Esser, and David Hopmann, 131–149. New York: Routledge.

Rövekamp, Ingmar. 2014. "Public Service Broadcasting in an International Comparison." *CESifo DICE Report* 12 (3): 51–53.

Scott, D. K., and R. H. Gobetz. 1992. "Hard News/Soft News Content of the National Broadcast Networks, 1972–1987." *Journalism Quarterly* 69 (2): 406–412.

Shehata, A. 2013. "Active or Passive Learning from Television? Political Information Opportunities and Knowledge Gaps during Election Campaigns." *Journal of Elections, Public Opinion and Parties* 23 (2): 200–222.

Sinardet, D., K. De Swert, and R. Dandoy. 2004. *Franstalig, Vlaams, commercieel, openbaar: Zoek de verschillen: Een longitudinale vergelijking van de thema's in de Belgische televisiejournaals* [French, Flemish, commercial, public: Find the differences: A longitudinal comparison of topics in Belgian television news]. Antwerpen: UA, Faculteit Politieke en Sociale Wetenschappen.

Soroka, S., B. Andrew, T. Aalberg, S. Iyengar, J. Curran, S. Coen, Kaori Hayashi, P. Jones, G. Mazzoleni, J. W. Rhee, D. Rowe, and R. Tiffen. 2013. "Auntie Knows Best? Public Broadcasters and Current Affairs Knowledge." *British Journal of Political Science* 43 (4): 719–739.

Strömbäck, J. 2015. "Learning Political News from Television: Comparing Knowledge Effects of Watching Public Service and Commercial TV News." Paper presented at the ECREA 2015 Political Communication Conference, Odense, Denmark, August 27–28.

Tracey, M. 1988. *The Decline and Fall of Public Service Broadcasting.* Oxford: Oxford University Press.

van Santen, R., and R. Vliegenthart. 2013. "TV Programming in Times of Changing Political Communication: A Longitudinal Analysis of the Political Information Environment." *European Journal of Communication* 28 (4): 397–419.

Waldahl, R., M. B. Andersen, and H. Rønning. 2009. *TV-nyhetenes verden* [The world of television news]. Oslo: Universitetsforlaget.

3

The Impact of Austerity on the Greek News Media and Public Sphere

Aristotelis Nikolaidis

Capitalism, Crisis and the Media

The case of contemporary Greece demonstrates that despite the ongoing capitalist crisis, neoliberalism has been entrenched rather than discredited. According to Hall, Massey and Rustin, 'the burden of "solving" the crisis has been disproportionately off-loaded on to working people, targeting vulnerable, marginalised groups' and has served as an excuse for the 'further restructuring of state and society along market lines, with a raft of ideologically-driven "reforms" designed to advance privatisation and marketisation' (2015, 4–5).

The dynamic of change unleashed in the context of capitalist crises concomitantly involves significant ideological and institutional shifts in the field of politics and culture (Harvey 2014, ix). The media system is central to this very process, as media portrayals constitute how the 'reality' of the crisis is constructed, mapped out and contextualized. This chapter addresses such recent shifts within the Greek media system in relation to its political role, the breadth of opinions represented and the open spaces it provides to alternative views. It also discusses some examples from my research on the representation of the crisis in Greece from 2011 to 2015, which is part of a project addressing media coverage of crisis in the European Union (Nikolaidis 2015a, 2015b, 2016).

Public Communication during the Crisis: The Greek Case

The effects of the crisis on the media field may be seen as being driven by a combination of polarization and fragmentation. It is characterized by three key developments: First, the chief tendency of the mainstream, privately owned and market-driven media has been to provide ideological legitimacy to the so-called memorandum/bailout agreements, the policies of austerity stemming from them and the political elites implementing them.

Second, although mainstream Greek journalism sustained and reproduced the hegemonic neoliberal agenda (Doudaki 2015; Mylonas 2014), a simultaneous counter-tendency has emerged: the growth of a multitude of alternative news outlets, mostly online. These have been a source of critical views on the memorandum policies. Katalipsi ESIEA, the blog of the 2009 occupation of the Athenian Union of Journalists headquarters (Siapera, Papadopoulou, and Archontakis 2014), is a typically radical example highlighting, among other things, the impact of austerity in the form of redundancies and exploitative precarious labour in the Greek media industries.

Third is the closing down of the public broadcaster ERT in 2013, a development which made the clash between the mainstream and alternative online news agendas all the more stark. ERT was abruptly shut down by the previous Conservative-led government as part of its policy of cuts. The staff occupied the headquarters and continued to broadcast online with the support of EBU and Greek alternative news websites until they were evicted by riot police. ERT was succeeded by a failed attempt to establish a new broadcaster and was eventually restored by the current government.

The closing down of ERT has been rightly seen as a blow to media pluralism (Iosifidis and Boucas 2015, 19), but it is also part of a wider set of pressures on journalists, including censorship, self-censorship, prosecution and police violence (Syllas 2013). As a result, the country has the European Union's second lowest ranking in the 2015 World Press Freedom Index, having fallen fifty-six places during the years of the crisis (Zikakou 2015).

The Political Economy of a Media Oligopoly

An analysis of public communication in such a context of crisis and change needs to take into account the ways in which major media organizations operate as privately owned and profit-orientated capitalist enterprises—not least of all because the Greek case is characterised by highly concentrated ownership across media sectors (Leandros 2010) and has often been seen as constituting a media oligopoly with connections to political elites (Iosifidis and Boucas 2015, 14). The existing concentration of media power is the outcome of major structural shifts in media ownership during the 1980s. Finance, originating mainly from the construction, shipping and oil industries, was then invested in the print media sector. Along with the remaining traditional publishers, private capital then gained control of broadcasting through the emergence of private television, which has remained practically unlicensed and unregulated (Nikolaidis 1999).

Furthermore, privately owned media organizations have accumulated severe levels of debt (Darzanou 2013). They largely operate through bank loans, into which a judicial inquiry was recently launched (Kitsios 2015), as well as through favourable treatment of their debt by pro-memorandum political elites (Papadopoulos 2013). Media debt characteristically includes more than €24 million of unpaid tax for the use of broadcasting frequencies during the 2011 to 2014 period. The overall picture is that private economic interests have achieved significant control over the public sphere in Greece under politically privileged and economically unhealthy terms. This is not to suggest that there is a deterministic, cause and effect type of relation between capitalist control of the media and journalistic content. It is, however, to suggest that the market is not neutral and that the economic aspects of media companies set the general limits of their operation. Thus, the activity of private and concentrated media ownership in a deregulated market is first and foremost a political issue, which threatens to undermine the quality of contemporary democracy (Nikolaidis 1999, 2008). This effect is characteristically demonstrated in the coverage of the economic crisis.

Mainstream Media and the Politics of Austerity

The Greek case reveals increasingly homogenised content appearing across the mainstream media, which has resulted in coherent support for the bailout agreements, the implementation of the neoliberal policies they involve and hostile coverage of opposition and critique by left-wing parties and movements.

The editorials and opinion columns of the mainstream newspapers *To Vima* and *Kathimerini*, ideologically positioned in the centre and the right respectively, are exemplary of this; they both share a distinctly ideological narrative that depoliticises the crisis by neutralizing its systemic character.

The crisis is discursively constructed as a national emergency, which demands a consensus response from all the major political parties (Kathimerini 2014a; To Vima 2011a) in order to avert imminent financial and social meltdown (Karakousis 2011). Under such terms, austerity is legitimized as an objective economic necessity and/or a necessary lesser evil (Mandravelis 2011). Unsurprisingly, economic recovery is often interpreted in explicitly pro-business terms. *To Vima* urges workers' unions to willingly succumb to wage losses so as to 'facilitate' industrialists in their activities (To Vima 2011b) and appeals to the patriotism of businessmen in the hope of turning Greece 'into a contemporary El Dorado' (To Vima 2012). *Kathimerini* celebrates both the identification of countries as brands (Kathimerini 2014b) and the equation of politics with management (Kathimerini 2014c).

The interpretation of the crisis in national terms constitutes the prevalence of consensus politics, which, at the same time, also manifests in mainstream media attacks on left-wing critics of the bailout agreements and austerity. In one characteristic example, the left is repeatedly addressed as 'loony' (Mandravelis 2012, 2015), in a fashion reminiscent of Thatcher-era British tabloids. The Greek case, however, is paradigmatic of a far more aggressive rhetorical strategy, the so-called 'theory of the two extremes', aiming to delegitimise the left by equating it with the violence of the Nazi party called Golden Dawn. In two notorious examples, this strategy was manifested in almost identical titles in different newspapers (Kasimatis 2012; Pretenteris 2012). Ironically, it was the mainstream media that contributed to the rise of the Nazi party amidst the crisis (Psarras 2012). Golden Dawn was whitewashed through high-profile interviews on private television (Horis Mantri 2015), and fake news was manufactured in its favour (Ios 2013). Just five days before the murder of the anti-fascist musician Pavlos Fyssas by Golden Dawn, which obliged authorities to begin long-overdue prosecutions of the party as a criminal organization, the party was still considered as a potential part of a conservative alliance (Papadimitriou 2013).

Alternative Media and Meta-Journalism

Such an overwhelmingly flawed performance of the media's democratic role was also displayed during the recent referendum on further austerity measures. The mainstream media were accused of fearmongering and bias in favour of the *yes* vote. Subsequently, the Athenian union of journalists referred nine prominent private television journalists to its disciplinary board. In two well-known Facebook posts that went viral, content analysis of television revealed the striking imbalance of coverage of the rallies for the *no* and the *yes* votes; the coverage strongly favoured the latter (Petropoulos 2015a, 2015b).

Alternative media has offered an important counter to the mainstream. In Greece, it is a multifaceted field consisting of independent websites and magazines, crowdfunded documentaries, digital radio stations and a thriving community of bloggers and social network users. It has been enriched by the online presence of anti-austerity groups, the antifascist movement, grassroots syndicalism and left-wing organizations. As a whole, this field represents key features of citizen journalism and includes an active tradition of open publishing.

However, it also has limitations. First, the emerging relationship between alternative news and social movements on the one hand and commercial social media platforms on the other displays the effectiveness but also the contradictions that characterize cases such as Occupy (Fuchs 2014). Second, the exploitation of digital platforms by the Nazi Golden Dawn party (Kompatsiaris and Mylonas 2015) remains a politically dangerous blind spot.

The political and journalistic implications of the emergence of bottom-up pressures online may be demonstrated in the case of Twitter, a platform on which the mainstream media have been given hashtags consisting of the names of private television stations and the slang word for 'disgraceful/ridiculous' (#mega_xeftiles, #skai_xeftiles, etc.). In one characteristic case, the trending hashtag 'flying anarchists' (#iptamenoi_anarxikoi) was used to effectively ridicule and contradict the coverage of clashes between police and protestors on the private television channel Ant1. The Ant1 reporter claimed to have access to exclusive information about, among other things, an 'airborne anarchist brigade', and he was eventually held accountable by the online community for his adoption of the perspective of the police (Lefteria, 2014). This example demonstrates the potential of challenging official definitions and contesting the power of sources from below. At the same time, however, it also demonstrates that despite important meta-journalistic victories against the mainstream media, such media maintain their dominant reach towards large audiences, and that official power holders continue to enjoy privileged access to them.

Austerity, Consensus Politics and the Media System

The multi-layered economic, political and social changes driven by the current crisis pose continuous challenges to the political role of the media system. Current ideological and institutional shifts suggest the formation of an unprecedented elite political consensus in support of the neoliberal restructuring of Greek society. Pivotal to this development has been the shift of the SYRIZA-led government away from its anti-austerity electoral platform and its endorsement of a third memorandum agreement to more austerity measures and privatizations. Perhaps more importantly, however, the prevailing consensus has also entrenched national narratives. These frame the crisis in terms of an opposition between Greece and powerful EU member states such as Germany, at the expense of a critique of neoliberalism and class politics both in Greece and across the EU.

At the same time, the government has embarked on a broadcast license auction (Sweney 2016), the outcome of which remains uncertain at the time of writing; it nonetheless appears to aim at changing the composition of the capitalist interests controlling a now reduced number of private television stations, rather than placing barriers to concentrated media ownership in the public interest and empowering the regulation of broadcasting through an independent public authority. The extent to which alternative online media may be able to contest the impact of market-driven media organizations and rejuvenate public communication in an era of consensus politics remains to be seen. However, the implementation of austerity as a principle means of devaluing labour power and redistributing wealth towards capital depends upon the disciplining of the affected workforce and the ideological assimilation of opposition. Thus, the direct connection between the economics and the politics of the crisis suggests that law and order news remains a key media topic necessary for contesting official definitions.

References

Darzanou, A. 2013. "Seeking 'Total Solutions' to the Media's Financial Losses and Debt [in Greek]." *Avgi*, December 28. http://www.avgi.gr/article/1574218/ anazitountai-%C2%ABsunolikes-luseis%C2%BB-gia-tis-zimies-kai-ta-xrei -ton-mme.

Doudaki, V. 2015. "Legitimation Mechanisms in the Bailout Discourse." *Javnost—The Public* 22 (1): 1–17.

Fuchs, C. 2014. *OccupyMedia! The Occupy Movement and Social Media in Crisis Capitalism.* Winchester, UK: Zero Books.

Hall, S., D. Massey, and M. Rustin. 2015. "After Neoliberalism: Analysing the Present." In *After Neoliberalism? The Kilburn Manifesto*, edited by S. Hall, D. Massey, and M. Rustin, 9–23. London: Lawrence and Wishart Limited.

Harvey, D. 2014. *Seventeen Contradictions and the End of Capitalism.* London: Profile Books.

Horis Mantri. 2015. "#GDtrial Golden Dawn did not arose from nowhere. It was whitewashed by small-time agents who pretend to be saviors today https://www.youtube.com/watch?v=1P7HVQWj7zE ... [in Greek]." Twitter, April 19. https://twitter.com/Agapi_V/status/589829527938949120.

Ios. 2013. "This Is How the News about the Old Ladies Was Manufactured." *Efimerida Ton Syntakton*, September 23. http://archive.efsyn.gr/?p=118424.

Iosifidis, P., and D. Boucas. 2015. "Media Policy and Independent Journalism in Greece." Open Society Foundations, May 1. https://www.opensociety foundations.org/sites/default/files/media-policy-independent-journalism -greece-20150511.pdf.

Karakousis, A. 2011. "You Are to Blame if We Turn into Argentina [in Greek]!" *To Vima*, May 27. http://www.tovima.gr/opinions/article/?aid=403128&h1=true.

Kasimatis, S. 2012. "The Golden Dawn Opportunity for Democracy [in Greek]." *Kathimerini*, September 16. http://www.kathimerini.gr/731901/opinion/ epikairothta/arxeio-monimes-sthles/h-eykairia-ths-xryshs-ayghs-gia-th-dhmokratia.

Kathimerini. 2014a. "Consensus [in Greek]." *Kathimerini*, editorial, September. http://www.kathimerini.gr/783526/opinion/epikairothta/politikh/synaines.

Kathimerini. 2014b. "The Good Name of Greece [in Greek]." *Kathimerini*, editorial, May 4. http://www.kathimerini.gr/765414/opinion/epikairothta/ politikh/to-kalo-onoma-ths-elladas.

Kathimerini. 2014c. "The Most Capable Managers [in Greek]." *Kathimerini*, editorial, May 11. http://www.kathimerini.gr/766577/opinion/epikairothta/ politikh/toys-pio-ikanoys-manatzer.

Kitsios, C. 2015. "Prosecutor Inquiry into Loans to the Press [in Greek]!" *euro2day*, April 3. http://www.euro2day.gr/news/economy/article/1320208/ eisaggelikh-erevna-gia-ta-daneia-ston-typo.html.

Kompatsiaris, P., and Y. Mylonas. 2015. "The Rise of Nazism and the Web: Social Media as Platforms of Racist Discourses in the Context of the Greek Economic Crisis." In *Social Media, Politics and the State: Protests, Revolutions, Riots, Crime, and Policing in the Age of Facebook, Twitter and YouTube*, edited by C. Fuchs and D. Trottier, 109–130. New York: Routledge.

Leandros, N. 2010. "Media Concentration and Systemic Failures in Greece." *International Journal of Communication* 4:886–905.

Lefteria. 2014. "The #flying Reporter Karaivaz Replies about Ant1's Whitewashing and #iptamenoi_anarxikoi [in Greek]." *Lefteria*, December 9. https://lefterianews.wordpress.com/2014/12/09/%CE%BF-%CE%B9%CF%80 %CF%84%CE%B1%CE%BC%CE%AD%CE%BD%CE%BF%CF%82-%CF%81%C E%B5%CF%80%CF%8C%CF%81%CF%84%CE%B5%CF%81-%CE%BA%CE%B1 %CF%81%CE%B1%CF%8A%CE%B2%CE%AC%CE%B6-%CE%B1%CF%80%CE %B1%CE%BD%CF%84%CE%AC/.

Mandravelis, P. 2011. "A Big Thank You [in Greek]." *Kathimerini*, June 30. http://www.kathimerini.gr/725803/opinion/epikairothta/arxeio-monimes -sthles/ena-megalo-eyxaristw.

Mandravelis, P. 2012. "Surplus of Irrationalism [in Greek]." *Kathimerini*, November 24. http://www.kathimerini.gr/20479/opinion/epikairothta/politikh/pleonasma-paralogismoy.

Mandravelis, P. 2015. "Complex-Ridden Left [in Greek]." *Kathimerini*, July 3. http://www.kathimerini.gr/822091/opinion/epikairothta/politikh/komple3ikh-aristera.

Mylonas, Y. 2014. "Crisis, Austerity and Opposition in Mainstream Media Discourses of Greece." *Critical Discourse Studies* 11 (3): 305–321.

Nikolaidis, A. 1999. "The Media under Restrictive Legislation: The Case of the Greek Press in the Early 1990s." PhD diss., Goldsmiths College, University of London.

Nikolaidis, A. 2008. "Democracy and the Political Role of the Media: The Case of the Greek Press in the Early 1990s." Paper presented at Anniversary Conference: Media, Communication & Humanity, London School of Economics and Political Science, September 21–23.

Nikolaidis, A. 2015a. "Immigration and the 2015 Election: The Banal, the Racist, and the Unspoken." In *UK Election Analysis 2015: Media, Voters and the Campaign*, edited by D. Jackson and E. Thorsen, 98. Poole, UK: Centre for the Study of Journalism, Culture and Community, Bournemouth University. http://www.electionanalysis.uk/.

Nikolaidis, A. 2015b. "Mediating the State of Exception? Neoliberalism, Immigration and the Media amidst the Greek Crisis." Paper presented at Reframing Media/Cultural Studies in the Age of Global Crisis, University of Westminster, June 19–20.

Nikolaidis, A. 2016. "Communities in Crisis: Mediating Austerity and the Politics of Suicide." Paper presented at the Annual MeCCSA Conference 2016: Communities, Canterbury Christ Church University, Canterbury, UK, January 6–8.

Papadimitriou, B. 2013. "Annoying Confrontations [in Greek]." *Kathimerini*, September 13. http://www.kathimerini.gr/736781/opinion/epikairothta/arxeio-monimes-sthles/enoxlhtikes-antipara8eseis.

Papadopoulos, K. 2013. "Gift [worth] millions to [television] channel owners [in Greek]." *The Press Project*, January 13. http://www.thepressproject.gr/article/36529/Xarizontai-gia-3i-fora-ekatommuria-euro-stous-kanalarxes.

Petropoulos, M. 2015a. "A Deeper Look into MEGA News [in Greek]." Facebook status update, June 30. https://www.facebook.com/photo.php?fbid=88897221 4507411&set=a.104973436240630.8199.100001839227705&type=1.

Petropoulos, M. 2015b. "On Objectivity (Part 2) [in Greek]." Facebook status update, July 2. https://www.facebook.com/photo.php?fbid=889712667766699 &set=a.104973436240630.8199.100001839227705&type=1.

Pretenteris, G. 2012. "Golden Opportunity [in Greek]." *To Vima*, September 16. http://www.tovima.gr/opinions/article/?aid=475049.

Psarras, D. 2012. *The Black Book of Golden Dawn: Documents on the History and Actions of a Nazi Group [in Greek]*. Athens: Polis.

Siapera, E., L. Papadopoulou, and F. Archontakis. 2014. "Post-crisis Journalism: Critique and Renewal in Greek Journalism." *Journalism Studies* 16 (3): 449–465.

Sweney, M. 2016. "Greece Cuts TV Channels from Eight to Four in Controversial License Auction." *The Guardian*, September 2. https://www .theguardian.com/media/2016/sep/02/greece-tv-channels-licence-auction.

Syllas, C. 2013. "Free Speech Takes a Beating." *Index on Censorship* 42 (1): 16–20.

To Vima. 2011a. "Consensus Now [in Greek]!" *To Vima*, editorial, May 13. http://www.tovima.gr/opinions/article/?aid=400636.

To Vima. 2011b. "The 'Pirelli' Syndrome [in Greek]." *To Vima*, editorial, December 17. http://www.tovima.gr/opinions/article/?aid=435249&h1=true.

To Vima. 2012. "Will Businessmen Show Up [in Greek]?" *To Vima*, editorial, November 10. http://www.tovima.gr/opinions/article/?aid=483214.

Zikakou, I. 2015. "Greece Ranks 91st in World Press Freedom Index." *Greek Reporter*, February 19. http://greece.greekreporter.com/2015/02/19/ greece-ranks-91st-in-world-press-freedom-index/.

4

Impoverishing the Mediated Public Sphere in Aotearoa-New Zealand: The Slow Demise of Television News and Current Affairs

Wayne Hope

The last episode of TV3's *Campbell Live* on May 29, 2015, signalled the end of primetime current affairs on New Zealand television. In many ways, its demise also marks the end of the once thriving mediated public sphere that had developed in the country since the 1960s, to be replaced by a set of transnational, financialized corporations with market goals.

Campbell Live succeeded in spite of the prevailing conditions. Today in New Zealand, apart from the Māori Television Network (established in 2004), free-to-air channels are saturated with tabloid infotainment shows, sponsored reality TV formats, advertising segments and product placements. Interviews with public figures and issues-based reporting were consigned to early morning weekend slots. Against the trend, *Campbell Live* began on March 21, 2005, at 7 pm with Carol Hirschfield as producer and John Campbell as presenter/correspondent/reporter. The show was always a hybrid. Interviews with politicians and public figures and issue-driven stories mingled with lighter infotainment pieces and programme sponsorship. The then owner of TV3 and sister channel TV4, Canada's Canwest media conglomerate, exemplified the North American model of commercial television. Each successful network required a high-profile news brand and news presenter to push prime-time ratings. John Campbell was TV3's major identity and investment. The rise and fall of *Campbell Live*, amidst a changing media landscape, reflects the worsening plight of primetime current affairs television and the mediated public sphere.

Roll back a few decades, to before the neoliberal policy shifts of the Labour government in the 1980s, and the country was experiencing a thriving public sphere. My conception of the *public sphere* includes guaranteed freedoms of association, expression and publication and their independence from arbitrary state power, religious authority and private commercial interests. Actually existing public spheres of communication within legal environments, artistic and literary communities, political parties, representative institutions, universities and media domains can be outlined *and* evaluated against their own implicit value claims (Habermas 1992; Hope 2012). Based on these criteria, a nationally mediated public sphere emerged in the 1960s and 1970s.

In the context of a Keynesian social democratic polity and a Westminster two-party system, a semi-independent network—the New Zealand Broadcasting Corporation (NZBC)—was established in 1961, thus ending formal ministerial control of the airwaves and initiating a new relationship among government, broadcasting and journalism. Although NZBC bureaucrats were paternalistic, broadcasting journalists were, for the first time, able to interpret political issues (Cleveland 1969). Radio programmes such as *In the News*, *Checkpoint* and *Viewpoint* introduced listeners to political commentary. On the NZBC's single television channel, the current affairs programme *Gallery*, fronted by Brian Edwards, challenged government ministers and criticized official institutions, such as the police and the Security Intelligence Service. In 1973, the year after Labour gained office, a new Broadcasting Act further enhanced the autonomy of broadcast journalism. The Broadcasting Ministry portfolio was abolished and replaced by a seven-member council presiding over Radio New Zealand (RNZ) and a competitive two-channel, colour television network, forming a public broadcasting system loosely based on the BBC model.

Although the national government of 1975 introduced a new Broadcasting Act to reduce the institutional autonomy of Television New Zealand (TVNZ) and RNZ, governments could no longer manage news independently of news professionals. The stock figures of journalists and politicians were at the foreground of mediated public life. Audiences became accustomed to interview formats and adversarial debate over economic, social and foreign policy. Television programmes such as *Close Up*, *Dateline Monday*, and *News at 10* combined interviews, studio discussion formats and investigative pieces (Hope 2012).

Over the same period, newspapers from the four major centres—Dunedin, Christchurch, Wellington and Auckland—advanced the range and depth of news coverage. The New Zealand Press Association (NZPA), a conservative newsgathering organization, was complemented by the Parliamentary Press Gallery. Each major newspaper had between one and six journalists reporting daily. Outside of controversial issues, gallery correspondents provided day-to-day coverage of parliament, along with reports on farming, commerce, industry, finance and public administration. Although such journalism was not critical or investigative, the available range of commentary was extended. In some newspapers and magazines, such as *The Listener*, enterprising journalists could tackle volatile topics, such as race relations, youth culture and protest activism.

Thus, the 1960s and 1970s saw the emergence of a nationally mediated public sphere shaped by a semi-independent broadcasting system, a modern commercial press, and current affairs journalism. Meanwhile, traditional constructions of national identity, which had shaped the officially mediated public sphere, were challenged by new social movements. Most importantly, against the backdrop of white settler capitalism, a Māori cultural resurgence and an associated struggle for land rights openly contradicted the colony-to-nation progress myth upon which kiwi national identity had been founded. Second-wave feminists, green activists, anti–Vietnam War protestors and an anti-apartheid movement opposed to sporting ties with White South Africa also challenged conventional notions of 'New Zealand-ness'. The political issues of women's reproduction rights, equal pay, New Zealand's involvement in US military interventions, forest and lake conservation and All Black rugby contacts with South Africa dominated news and current affairs. Māori land occupations, women's conventions, protests against US dignitaries, South African sports teams and environmentally destructive energy projects were national media events.

From 1984, under neoliberal policies introduced by the Fourth Labour Government, broadcasting was deregulated and media communication infrastructures were absorbed by transnational corporations. TVNZ and RNZ were turned into dividend-gathering, state-owned enterprises (1989). The entry of Sky, a subscription television network, allowed its subsequent principal shareholder, News Corporation, to acquire live match rights for major sporting codes: rugby union, rugby league, cricket, netball and English premier league soccer. The concurrent entry of TV3, as a regionally owned private television network, was initially unprofitable, and local shareholders went bankrupt. As of 1994, the new principal shareholders were Canadian media conglomerate Canwest (10 percent), Westpac Bank (48 percent) and an official receiver (32 percent) (Rosenberg 1994). Canwest was then Canada's largest media corporation, with film, print, television and other offshore holdings in Ireland, Northern Ireland, the United States and Australia. Between 1996 and 2000, it assumed control of the consortium running TV3 (and later TV4) and acquired a raft of commercial radio stations. In 1990, New Zealand's telecommunications infrastructure was sold to Bell Atlantic and Ameritech (34.2 percent each) along with local banks and businesses. The following year, under a national government even more committed to neoliberalism, all restrictions on foreign media ownership were lifted.

During the 1990s and early 2000s, transnational media communication conglomerates continued to colonise the mediated public sphere (Hope 2012). The effects upon broadcast news journalism and current affairs were multiple and long-lasting. Soon after broadcasting deregulation, Radio New Zealand management received 15 percent salary cuts, and other staff either lost overtime rates of pay or entered part-time contracts. At TVNZ, intense competition with TV3 for advertising revenue resulted in major layoffs across news desks and among production staff. In December 1990, regional news services in Christchurch and Dunedin were removed, as were Sunday night news shows (Scott 1995).

In the case of prime-time television news bulletins, a team of American news consultants transformed the existing format into infotainment packages. The central purpose was to build and maintain ratings flow between advertising segments. Content analysis undertaken by Joe Atkinson for the period between 1985 and 1992 demonstrated a marked decline in item length and a prevalence of brief sound bites. Emphasis shifted from issues relating to politics, economics, public policy and industrial relations to those of crime, human interest and natural disaster (Atkinson 1994). Daniel Cook's analysis of TVNZ's *One Network News* from 1984 to 1996 found that the average news item length fell from ninety to seventy seconds, and commercial breaks increased from 12 percent to 23 percent of the entire bulletin (Cook 2001).

The style and content of television current affairs on TVNZ and TV3 also changed markedly. Sarah Baker's analysis of such programmes from 1984 to 2004 indicates a diminishing item length and a 'significant decline in the coverage of serious political and informational subjects and a sustained and measurable move to more entertainment-oriented current affairs programmes' (Baker 2012, 221). In 1984, on TVNZ's *Sunday* and *Close Up* programmes, median item lengths were 19.1 and 16.0 minutes, respectively. By 2004, *Sunday's* median figure was 13.3 minutes. In 1994, five years after TVNZ introduced the magazine-style *Holmes* show, its median item length was a paltry 5.7 minutes (ibid., 129). This long-running programme, fronted by media personality Paul Holmes, encapsulated the growing prevalence of tabloid formats. Baker's research also indicated an increase in crime, celebrity, human interest, and other entertainment-oriented stories. In 1994, *Holmes* and TV3's *20/20* devoted 45 percent and 56 percent respectively of programme time to such content. By 2004, these figures had risen to 62 percent and 79 percent (ibid., 146).

Within this unforgiving commercial environment, *Campbell Live* from its inception developed a real national presence. A public sphere ethos drove stories about security service surveillance, environmental pollution, public health, declining real wages, overcrowded housing, and New Zealand residency scams. Ordinary citizens spoke straight to the camera, without the elaborate formatting typical of infotainment and reality TV shows. *Campbell Live*'s resilience in a non-public-service setting was truly remarkable.

However, the show's future became problematic starting in 2007, when Canwest sold its 70 percent stake in Mediaworks to HT Media, a subsidiary of the Australian private equity firm Ironbridge Capital for NZ$790 million. This exemplified a new financialized phase in the transnational colonization of domestic media. Mediaworks was the holding company for TV3, TV4 and a nationwide stable of commercial radio stations. After the 2008 global financial collapse and global recession, falling advertising revenues worsened Mediaworks' financial position. In 2009, it posted a NZ$314 million loss (Mollgaard and Rosenberg 2010). Subsequently, Ironbridge swapped its own financial debt for equity injections from Goldman Sachs, the Royal Bank of Scotland (RBS) and Bank of New Zealand (BNZ). By mid-2012, Mediaworks' debt restructuring involved two new major debt holders: TPG Capital and Oaktree Capital Management. The latter group bought NZ$125 million worth of Mediaworks' debt from the RBS and BNZ. By late 2013, Mediaworks was owned by Oaktree Capital (26.7 percent), RBS (21.9 percent), TPG Capital (15.7 percent), Westpac (14.6 percent), Rabobank (14.6 percent) and J. P. Morgan (6.5 percent; Myllylahti 2012). Oaktree Capital raised its ownership stake to 43 percent in 2014 and 100 percent in May 2015. With these developments,

Campbell Live was in mortal danger; short-term financial imperatives required a new business model for TV3.

Julie Christie, Mark Weldon and other Mediaworks managers favoured multi-platform broadcasting, low-cost reality TV shows and infotainment programmes with a skeletal staffing structure. The phrase *current affairs* would be maintained to obscure the objectives of restructuring and to taint *Campbell Live*'s accomplishments as a dated, tiresome form of the genre. In the latter context, a New Zealand Herald report on May 23, 2015 (Nippert and Thompson 2015) reported: 'Mediaworks management viewed *Campbell Live*'s crusading journalism as a liability that stretched viewer patience'. The report described ongoing coverage of the November 2010 Pike River coalmine explosion and resulting controversies as a cause of viewer 'fatigue' and criticised the emphasis given to 'the aftermath of the Christchurch earthquake', 'GCSB spying' and 'child poverty'.

The eventual demise of *Campbell Live* marked the end of a historical trajectory. State-run broadcasting without current affairs formats lasted from the early 1920s until around 1960. The subsequent development of a semi-independent broadcasting system fostered a culture of television journalism based on public sphere principles. New Zealand's neoliberal policy revolution, broadcasting deregulation and the transnational corporate absorption of national media reshaped television news and current affairs such that tabloid-infotainment formats prevailed. The financialisation of media ownership generally and of Mediaworks in particular completes the trajectory. After *Campbell Live*, Māori Television's *Native Affairs* is all that remains of prime-time current affairs. Yes, there is the Internet and a thriving political blogosphere and an advertising-free, though cash-strapped, radio national network in which public issues are debated. However, the commercially blasted television landscape has impoverished the journalistic public sphere.

References

Atkinson, J. 1994. "The State, the Media and Thin Democracy." In *Into the Dark: The Changing Role of the State in New Zealand since 1984*, edited by A. Sharp, 146–177. Auckland: Auckland University Press.

Baker, S. 2012. "The Changing Face of Current Affairs Television Programmes in New Zealand 1984–2004." PhD diss., School of Communication Studies, Auckland University of Technology.

Cleveland, L. 1969. "The New Zealand Mass Media System: Functions and Responsibilities." *Political Science* 21 (2): 36–47.

Cook, D. 2001. "Deregulation and Broadcast News Content: One Network News from 1984 to 1996." In *New Zealand Television: A Reader*, edited by J. Farnsworth and I. Hutchinson, 139–144. Palmerston North: Dunmore Press.

Habermas, J. 1992. *Structural Transformation of the Public Sphere*. Translated by T. Burger and P. Lawrence. Cambridge: Polity.

Hope, W. 2012. "New Thoughts on the Public Sphere in Aotearoa New Zealand." In *Scooped: The Politics and Power of Journalism in New Zealand*, edited by M. Hirst, S. Phelan, and V. Rupar, 27–47. Auckland: Auckland University of Technology Press.

Mollgaard, M., and B. Rosenberg. 2010. "Who Owns Radio in New Zealand?" *Communication Journal of New Zealand* 11 (1): 85–107.

Myllylahti, M. 2012. "New Zealand Media Ownership Report." Centre for Journalism, Media and Democracy (JMAD), Auckland University of Technology, Auckland.

Nippert, M., and W. Thompson. 2015. "Campbell's Crusades Irked TV3 Bosses." *New Zealand Herald*, May 23.

Rosenberg, B. 1994. "News Media Ownership in Aotearoa." *The Word*, July–August, 6.

Scott, J. M. 1995. "Neo-liberalism at Work: Media Politics and the Employment Contracts Act." MA thesis, University of Auckland.

5

Public-Commercial Hybridity at BBC News Online: Covering Non-governmental Organisations in Africa

Kate Wright

BBC News Online is one of the most popular news websites in the world (Jones and Salter 2011), with enormous credibility in the United Kingdom (Hendy 2013) and overseas, especially in the United States (Bicket and Wall 2009; Thurman 2007). It sits at the heart of the BBC's broader efforts to respond to the challenges of commercialisation, digitalisation and convergence, whilst remaining mindful of its commitment to public service values (Allan and Thorsen 2010; Thorsen, Allan, and Carter 2010). Yet serious concerns have been raised by Goldsmiths researchers about the ways in which the increased webcentricity of the corporation's journalism has been shaped by its executives' privileging of speed, technology and the homogeneity produced by recycling journalistic content (Lee-Wright 2010; Redden and Witschge 2010), now comprising part of a broader shift within the BBC towards marketised values.

My work (Wright 2015) serves to develop this research, as well as that carried out by Phillips into online journalists' changing sourcing practices (Phillips 2010). This is because my research found that the pressure to increase advertising revenue via the international-facing English-language site (BBC-News.com), together with the cost-cutting carried out before and after the licence fee freeze in 2010 (Hendy 2013; Tumber 2011), began to alter journalists' approach to sourcing and other forms of production practice. However, traditional Reithian values have not been marginalised by the intrusion of marketised norms. Instead, normative and economic values were found to modify one another via journalists' deliberative decision-making in ways that prompted journalists to reconstruct their approach to public service journalism.

The cases I examined involved journalists' use of multimedia provided by non-governmental organisations (NGOs) in the news coverage of Africa. However, in the course of conducting semi-structured interviews with those who made key decisions that shape the production of the two media items in question (Copnall and Hegarty 2011; Crowley and Fleming 2010[1]), it became clear that this relatively narrowly focused study had significant implications for the study of the corporation's broader engagement in different forms of public-commercial hybridity (Born 2004; Steemers 1999, 2005). In particular, it raises serious questions about the extent to which these internal and external changes are eroding the organisational policies and structures put in place historically by senior BBC executives to separate commercial from editorial decision-making.

An 'Absolute Divide between Church and State'?

In a rarely granted interview, Mark Byford, the former deputy director general of the BBC, explained that BBC News

Online was not initially conceptualised by senior managers as a money-making venture (Byford 2014). However, the rapid increase in the site's international audience, especially after the bombing of the World Trade Center in 2001 and the London Underground in 2005, led Byford to decide to allow advertising on BBCNews.com (Byford 2014). Although this was legitimised in terms of fairness to licence fee payers, Richard Sambrook, who was the head of Global News at the time, stressed that BBC executives had also hoped that the income raised by BBC News Online would help them pay for the soaring costs of international coverage and for further digital expansion (Sambrook 2014). In particular, he emphasized that executives hoped that advertising revenue would be significant enough to allow them to divert the Foreign Office Grant-in-Aid (which at the time was funding the international-facing section of the website, as well as World Service Radio) to Arabic satellite TV, because the Iraq war had led to this area being 'a big priority' for the corporation (Sambrook 2014).

However, Byford was eager that 'public trust in the authority of the BBC's journalism' should not be endangered by perceived threats to journalists' political impartiality and editorial independence (Byford 2014). Therefore, he tasked Sambrook with chairing a special committee of senior executives, whose responsibility was to establish organisational structures and policies in order to 'ensure a clear divide' between editorial and commercial decision-making (Byford 2014). Sambrook spoke rather more frankly about this; he argued that there had been 'enormous' internal tensions between the senior journalists at BBC News and the commercial executives at BBC Worldwide, who he said 'thought they could make a fortune' from the site but didn't understand the editorial and political 'sensitivities' involved and thus needed formal structures and policies in place to 'keep them honest' (Sambrook 2014).

For these reasons, the committee worked with the BBC Trust in order to pass organisational policy that placed the journalists at BBC News firmly in charge of all editorial commissioning, as well as clarifying where adverts could and could not be placed and specifying which kinds of adverts were appropriate (Sambrook 2014). The latter responsibility included banning adverts from NGOs, along with all other 'political . . . lobby or pressure groups', following a test case relating to Oxfam (BBC 2009, 10).

Nevertheless, large quantities of NGO-provided photos were found on BBC News Online in 2012. The placement of NGO photos on the site was indirectly shaped by serious changes to the BBC's political economy: In March 2010, Mark Thompson, then the BBC's director general, decided to cut the budget for BBC News Online by 25 percent. This was a 'tactical move' to try and ward off attacks by the corporation's commercial rivals and by the pro-market Conservative party, which looked likely to win the general election in May (Franklin 2012, 7). The strategy didn't work, and the licence fee freeze announced by the new Conservative-led coalition government led to the BBC experiencing a 16 percent drop in income in real terms, compounding the effects of earlier cuts at BBC News Online.

As David Moody, the head of strategy at BBC Worldwide, explained, the revenue generated by advertising placed on BBCNews.com is 'but a drop in the ocean' compared to the amount generated by licence fees, but finding ways to increase it became increasingly important to the corporation after 2010 (Moody 2014a). Because of the pressure to raise advertising income, BBC Worldwide began to make some editorial decisions, starting with commercial executives' engagement in 'rejigging' visuals and running orders, in order to 'represent content so that it is more relevant to international audiences' (Moody 2014a). Soon this 'representation' began to involve BBC World-wide commissioning 'supplementary content' for international audiences, albeit 'in consultation' with BBC News (Moody 2014a). This appears to undermine the organisational separa-tion of editorial and commercial decision-making agreed upon historically by Sambrook's committee, even though Moody maintained that there was still an 'absolute divide between Church and State' (Moody 2014a).

The editorial direction taken by BBC Worldwide executives also merits further research, because Moody described his pri-ority as commissioning the kinds of 'up-beat' lifestyle features that advertisers would like to 'associate their brand' with (Moody 2014a). These included items 'around Business, around Finance, around Health and Well-being, around Motoring... All the things that in their extreme form would be in what *The Financial Times* publishes in "How to Spend" on a Saturday' (Moody 2014a).

However, Moody complained that BBC journalists simply didn't make enough of the kinds of features that would appeal to advertisers seeking to reach those kinds of markets, so he 'had to' spend money commissioning these features from 'the market' (Moody 2014b). Indeed, he stressed that these kinds of BBC Worldwide–commissioned features now comprise 'an in-creasingly large part—often the majority' of the features on BBC News.com (Moody 2014b).

NGO-Provided Multimedia and Public-Commercial Hybridity

No evidence was found that such commissioning processes shaped the use of NGO-provided multimedia directly. However, the privileging of 'feel-good' features that trickled down from senior managers, together with cost-cutting measures designed to stimulate the publication of larger numbers of features via the recycling of other BBC content, was important (Redden and Witschge 2010). The production of the first media item studied involved the incorporation of photos taken by the South Sudanese media collective, Woyee Film and Theatre Ltd, in a feature article (Copnall and Hegarty 2011), and this hinged on the decision-making of Stephanie Hegarty, a World Service journalist tasked with combing the radio station's English-language output for non-news material suitable for publication online.

Hegarty stressed that her personal views and practices had become more nuanced since gaining more experience in the coverage of Africa and that the BBC's use of NGO-provided multimedia online was continuing to change rapidly, especially since the Ebola crisis in West Africa (Hegarty 2015). However, at the time of sampling, Hegarty said that senior managers had simply said that the site 'needed more features', and she had noticed that positive 'human interest' features were particularly warmly received (Hegarty 2012).

Therefore, Hegarty did not see herself as deliberately selecting media items on the basis of their appeal to advertisers. Instead, she described herself as serving other commercial aims (Hegarty 2012), although these also helped make the site more 'advertiser-friendly' (Moody 2014a).

Such aims included supplying BBC News Online journalists with immediately appealing 'human interest' stories that would be popular with and 'fun to read' for audiences (Hegarty 2012; see also Sambrook, Terrington, and Levy 2013), as well as sourcing stories about more unusual actors and places in order to differentiate BBC News Online from its competitors and sourcing large amounts of high-quality, visually appealing material so that the site was immediately striking visually.

All of these considerations shaped Hegarty's decision to recycle media items about small African collectives and co-operatives, such as the South Sudanese NGO, Woyee Film and Theatre Industry Ltd. An online feature about this NGO formed the basis of the first production case study examined here (Copnall and Hegarty 2011). But the work of the collective had initially been the subject of an arts radio package, composed by the BBC's Sudan and South Sudan correspondent, James Copnall, so Hegarty said she had much of the editorial material she already needed (Hegarty 2012). Although she did go on to conduct one additional interview herself, she stressed that the interview's main purpose was to ask permission to use the NGO's photos, which she had seen displayed on the group's Facebook site and which were of an unusually high technical quality for an African NGO because of their own focus on media production (Hegarty 2012).

Hegarty relished the opportunity to represent the members of the NGO as adept film-makers, seeing this as striking a blow against stereotypical 'negative' and 'disempowering' representations of Africans by others (Hegarty 2012). In this way, she argued she was enabling the BBC's public service journalism to function as a form of Reithian education (Hegarty 2012). However, in her eagerness to prepare a story that would be appealing immediately to the site's readers, she focused upon the entrepreneurialism and technical expertise of the NGO to such an extent that she inadvertently marginalised its more alternative, communitarian values (Danis 2013).

Nevertheless, using photos provided by a smaller, African NGO was quite unusual at BBC News Online. Joseph Winter, the site's Africa editor, said that a much more common use of NGO-provided multimedia would be a compilation of photo slideshows using images provided by major international NGOs (INGOs), despite the BBC's ban on accepting adverts from them (Winter 2013). Yet again, a key consideration here was how to make the site immediately appealing and visually distinctive, although Winter linked this far more explicitly to advertising than Hegarty. As he explained: 'There has been, if not exactly *pressure*, then *talk* of experiments about advertisers, because . . . if there's a special event coming up then there's so many adverts around it. And if there's a special page, then . . . for example, banks operating in South Sudan, you know, the likes of them *may* like to advertise around that so the page has to *look* really snazzy' (Winter 2013).

The lack of many internal photographers at BBC News Online and budgetary constraints therefore drove Winter to use the photographs provided by INGOs, which were able and willing to hire experienced freelance photojournalists whom he 'could not afford to employ' himself (Winter 2013). The technical and aesthetic qualities of these photos also meant that such slideshows were often republished in 'special reports' of archived material, such as the item on which the second case study was based (Crowley and Fleming 2010). This media text was an audio slideshow about a former child soldier from South Sudan, which incorporated photos taken by a member of staff from Save the Children UK. Although Winter was uncomfortable about repeatedly reinforcing the definitional advantages enjoyed by INGOs in the construction of knowledge about Africa, like Hegarty, he justified his actions according to Reithian ideas about the educative purpose of the BBC's public service journalism. He claimed that his rapid re-versioning of INGO-provided photos for slideshows enabled him to cope with the loss of one team member in the rounds of cost-cutting that had taken place (Fenton 2010), arguing that then he could focus on 'the real public service . . . the real *journalism*', which he (re)defined as *breaking news* (Winter 2013).

Yet perhaps the most worrying way in which the use of NGO-provided multimedia functioned in the reconstruction of public service journalism at BBC News Online involved its role in entrenching the promotional culture that shaped journalists' relationships with each other and with their audiences (Davis 2013). Editorial discussions between colleagues not only had speeded up because of the loss of several BBC News Online journalists, but also had become laden with noticeably commercial norms. For example, Hegarty stressed that she had to pitch re-versioned material that would be immediately appealing to the journalists on the Africa page, because they were so busy that they wouldn't have the time or energy to engage in more than 'a quick sell' (Hegarty 2012).

Likewise, Lucy Fleming, the journalist working with Winter on the Africa page, described herself as 'pushing' or 'selling' stories to the editors of main news pages, who then 'sold' or 'promoted' these stories to audiences (Fleming 2012). Fleming then went on to explain that INGO-provided multimedia was particularly useful in such processes, not only because it required little re-versioning (Fenton 2010), but also because INGOs usually had identified saleable events already, as well as stories about saleable individuals that would have significant emotional appeal to audiences (Fleming 2012; see also Davis 2013).

Indeed, Fleming even described a former child soldier, who appeared in the photos provided by Save the Children, as 'a really easy sell' (Fleming 2012). What was most interesting about this was the way in which Fleming blended even this heavily marketised approach with Reithian ideals in order to reconstruct her understanding of the normative purpose of public service journalism. She argued that the 'whole point' of such promotional processes was to try and get as many BBC News Online readers as possible to click on items about Africa, reasoning that then 'they should understand at least *some* of the issues involved' (Fleming 2012).

Conclusion

Although this study pertained specifically to the use of NGO-provided multimedia in the coverage of Africa provided by BBC News Online, it shows that journalists' sourcing and other production practices are changing due to the pressures exerted by both organisational cost-cutting and the need to generate more advertising revenue, both of which are linked to issues regarding audience popularity, market differentiation, speed and staffing. Further research clearly needs to be done in this area, but it appears that the intensity of such pressures has brought about the partial erosion of organisational structures designed historically to prevent the corporation's commercial aims from interfering with its journalists' editorial decision-making.

These findings build on previous work conducted at Goldsmiths regarding the marketisation of BBC News Online (Lee-Wright 2010; Redden and Witschge 2010), because they show that normative values are not necessarily marginalised in such processes. Rather, economic and normative values interact with and modify each other in the course of journalists' deliberative decision-making, transforming their approaches to public service journalism. The new, value-laden practices that emerge from these deliberations also have a complex relationship to homogeneity (Lee-Wright 2010; Redden and Witschge 2010): On the one hand, cash- and time-poor journalists used NGO-provided multimedia because they thought it would help them differentiate their content from other news outlets both visually and in terms of the people and places covered (Phillips 2010). But on the other hand, the kinds of content these journalists selected and the marketised ways in which they processed it tended to strip out its alterity.

Such changing production practices re-legitimise the BBC's reputation for offering a 'global' public news service, as well as enhance its ability to compete for audiences and advertisers online. However, this chapter raises serious questions about which and whose capabilities are enhanced by journalists' use of NGO-provided photos on BBC News Online. Therefore, this study speaks to current debates about the future funding of BBC journalism, demonstrating that organisational cost-cutting does not solely produce greater efficiency. Rather, it tends to produce unintended qualitative changes in what journalists do, how they do it and how they view the purpose/s of journalism. The risk is that these changes further marginalise the values and perspectives of those who are already disadvantaged and disempowered in the world.

Note

1. Both items were about South Sudan and appeared on the Africa page of BBC News Online during a single week in August 2012. However, the second item had been republished as part of a special collection of archived material to mark the first anniversary of the country's independence.

References

Allan, S., and E. Thorsen. 2010. "Journalism, Public Service and *BBC News Online*." In *News Online: Transformations and Continuities*, edited by G. Meikle and G. Redden, 20–37. Basingstoke, UK: Palgrave Macmillan.

BBC. 2009. "BBC Strategic Approval Committee." BBC Internal policy document, January 12.

Bicket, D., and M. Wall. 2009. "BBC News in the United States: A 'Super-alternative' News Medium Emerges." *Media, Culture & Society* 31 (3): 365–384.

Born, G. 2004. *Uncertain Vision: Birt, Dyke and the Reinvention of the BBC*. London: Secker & Warburg.

Byford, M. 2014. Telephone interview with author, February 5.

Copnall, J., and S. Hegarty. 2011. "Creating a Film Industry in South Sudan from Scratch." *BBC*, December 27. http://www.bbc.co.uk/news/world-africa-16319572.

Crowley, C., and L. Fleming. 2010. "Audio Slideshow: Ex-child Soldier in Sudan." *BBC*, April 5. http://news.bbc.co.uk/2/hi/africa/8599293.stm.

Danis, D. 2013. Telephone interview with author, February 20.

Davis, A. 2013. *Promotional Cultures: The Rise and Spread of Advertising, Public Relations, Marketing and Branding*. Cambridge: Polity Press.

Fenton, N. 2010. "NGOs, New Media and the Mainstream News: News from Everywhere." In *New Media, Old News: Journalism and Democracy in the Digital Age*, edited by N. Fenton, 153–168. London: Sage.

Fleming, L. 2012. In-person interview with author, November 16.

Franklin, B. 2012. "Introduction." In *The Future of Journalism, reprint edition*, edited by B. Franklin, 1–22. London: Routledge.

Hegarty, S. 2015. Email to author, May 11.

Hegarty, S. 2012. In-person interview with author, November 27.

Hendy, D. 2013. *Public Service Broadcasting*. New York: Palgrave Macmillan.

Jones, J., and L. Salter. 2011. *Digital Journalism*. London: Sage.

Lee-Wright, P. 2010. "Culture Shock: New Media and Organizational Change at the BBC." In *New Media, Old News: Journalism and Democracy in the Digital Age*, edited by N. Fenton, 71–86. London: Sage.

Moody, D. 2014a. Telephone interview with author, January 24.

Moody, D. 2014b. Email to author, February 17.

Phillips, A. 2010. "Old Sources, New Bottles." In *New Media, Old News: Journalism and Democracy in the Digital Age*, edited by N. Fenton, 87–101. London: Sage.

Redden, J., and T. Witschge. 2010. "A New News Order? Online News Content Examined." In *New Media, Old News: Journalism and Democracy in the Digital Age*, edited by N. Fenton, 171–186. London: Sage.

Sambrook, R. 2014. Telephone interview with author, April 14.

Sambrook, R., S. Terrington, and D. Levy. 2013. "The Public Appetite for Foreign News in TV and Online." Reuters Institute for the Study of Journalism, April. http://reutersinstitute.politics.ox.ac.uk/publication/public-appetite-foreign-news-tv-and-online.

Steemers, J. 1999. "Between Culture and Commerce: The Problem of Redefining Public Service Broadcasting for the Digital Age." *Convergence: The International Journal of Research into New Media Technologies* 5 (3): 44–66.

Steemers, J. 2005. "Balancing Culture and Commerce on the Global Stage." In *Cultural Dilemmas in Public Service Broadcasting*, edited by G. Lowe and J. Ferrelland Per, 213–250. Goteborg, Sweden: Nordicom.

Thorsen, E., S. Allan, and C. Carter. 2010. "Citizenship and Public Service: The Case of *BBC News Online*." In *Web Journalism: A New Form of Citizenship?*, edited by S. Tunney and G. Monahan, 116–125. Brighton: Sussex Academic Press.

Thurman, N. 2007. "The Globalization of Journalism Online: A Transatlantic Study of News Websites and Their International Readers." *Journalism: Theory, Practice and Criticism* 8 (3): 285–307.

Tumber, H. 2011. "Business as Usual: Enough of Phone Hacking, Let's Attack the BBC." *Television & New Media* 13 (1): 12–16.

Winter, J. 2013. In-person interview with author, May 7.

Wright, K. 2015. "A Quiet Revolution: The Moral Economies Shaping Journalists' Use of NGO-provided Multimedia in Mainstream News about Africa." PhD diss., Goldsmiths, University of London.

6

The New American Media Landscape

Rodney Benson

US journalism has taken a fresh turn in recent years. A small group of major digital commercial and non-profit news ventures seem to be here to stay, and they are providing real competition to the still dominant legacy media outlets. New and old media alike are creating new forms of civically valuable journalism, but in the shadow of increasingly concentrated and opaque economic wealth.

Since the 1990s, the US commercial journalistic field has sub-divided into three segments, all of them operating online and some with still substantial offline components: a mass infotainment segment consisting of well-established websites such as Yahoo!, BuzzFeed, Huffington Post and rising stars such as Vice and Vox, as well as local commercial television news; a partisan segment represented by (conservative) Fox and (left-liberal) MSNBC, mostly conservative talk radio, and the political blogosphere; and a 'mainstream' quality segment led by national newspapers such as the *New York Times* and *Wall*

Street Journal, the national network news and general news magazines such as *Time* and leading regional newspapers.

The boundaries between these categories are fluid (many outlets, including network television news and digital outlets such as Huffington Post and Vox, attempt to straddle the quality/mass divide) and often contested (conservative critics dismiss attempts by the *New York Times* and other mainstream media to present themselves as nonpartisan). Although audiences tend to concentrate in one of the three segments or sub-segments (in the case of partisan media, left or right, respectively), there is also some movement from one to the other through either conscious effort or social media–led serendipity. As I argue in this chapter, the small but dynamic US public and non-profit sectors mostly are *not* a counterforce to this market-based system, but rather supplement and increasingly cooperate with commercial outlets.

America's ongoing natural experiment can provide important lessons for the rest of the world: What new forms of journalism are US commercial and non-profit media bringing into being? How do these projects map to the demographics and media usage patterns of the citizenry? And what are the civic possibilities and limitations of this commercially dominated system?

Before we try to answer these questions, we need to set the stage by taking a closer look at the causes and consequences of the financial crisis that began in earnest in the mid-2000s and continues to shape the American journalistic field.

The Financial Crisis in American Journalism

The ongoing US journalistic financial crisis needs to be understood in relative terms. At least until around 2005, news media companies were among the most profitable companies in the United States, regularly earning 20 to 30 percent profit margins (O'Shea 2011). Media companies relied heavily on advertising for their revenues; American newspapers earned 80 percent of their revenues from advertising, the highest proportion in the world (WAN 2007).

The trade-off between this hyper-commercial logic and public service commitment was evident when Wall Street sent Knight-Ridder stock prices tumbling in 1986 on the day the newspaper chain won seven Pulitzer Prizes. Reportedly, Knight-Ridder executive Frank Hawkins phoned a stock analyst who followed the company to ask him why the shares had lost so much value: '"Because," he was told, "you win too many Pulitzers." The money spent on those projects, the analyst said, should be left to fall to the bottom line' (Meyer 2006, 6). Pressures continued to intensify during the 1990s as profit maximization came to dominate all other considerations.

It was in the midst of this less than idyllic situation that the crisis, or rather a series of crises, arrived after the dawn of the new century: notably, the decline of print classified and display advertising and their meagre replacement by online advertising, and the financial crises of 2001 and 2008, which further depressed advertising revenues. From the historic peak year of 2005 to 2013, advertising revenues for newspapers plummeted from $49 billion to just over $20 billion; only about 10 percent of the current total comes from digital advertising (Pew Research Center 2014b).

Despite the dramatic drop in revenues, newspaper companies have continued to maintain profits of 8 to 15 percent by digging ever deeper for newsroom cuts (Mitchell 2012). Over the past decade, full-time newspaper journalism jobs have been reduced from sixty thousand to forty thousand (Downie and Schudson 2009). In particular, public affairs reporting—especially investigative reporting—from the local to the international level has been hit especially hard (Walton 2010; Enda 2010).

Publicly traded companies, once the dominant form of newspaper ownership, are increasingly selling off major outlets to wealthy individuals, such as Amazon founder Jeff Bezos (*Washington Post*), Boston Red Sox owner John Henry (*Boston Globe*), Minnesota Timberwolves owner Glen Taylor (*Minneapolis Star-Tribune*) and conservative activist billionaire Sheldon Adelson (*Las Vegas Review-Journal*). The *Washington Post*, under Bezo's stewardship, has expanded and thrived; the *Las Vegas Review-Journal*, on the other hand, has been rocked by accusations of publisher political meddling. The new media moguls, even when they seem benevolent, raise new problems of transparency and accountability in the exercise of public power.

To address the shortcomings of the commercial system—what economists would call 'market failure' (Baker 2002)—in most other democracies, a logical step would be for the state to intervene in some way. But in the United States, a public policy solution is vigorously opposed by an uneasy coalition of anti-government conservatives and professional journalists, the latter motivated by a strict interpretation of the First Amendment, which they see as prohibiting any government involvement with the press.

Compared to any other leading democratic nation-state, the United States has the smallest taxpayer-funded public media sector by far. The pillars of this system are PBS (Public Broadcasting Service) and NPR (National Public Radio); public funding amounts to $4 (slightly less than €4) per capita, compared to $50 for the public service media of France, $91 for

Great Britain and $130 for Germany, Norway and Denmark. To be clear, PBS and NPR are public/non-profit 'hybrids': They receive the majority of their revenues from charitable donations, large and small. Yet even when these donations are added to the mix, the total funding of America's public media is still less than $10 per capita (Benson and Powers 2011).

The Online Pecking Order: Legacy Media Still Dominate

Despite the financial crisis and the downsizing of their journalistic mission and ambitions, it must be emphasized that 'legacy' commercial media (companies originally producing newspapers, magazines and/or television) continue to dominate the US media system in two market metrics: revenues/profits and online audiences.

The largest online-only news outlets, Huffington Post (ranked fourth in online monthly unique users) and BuzzFeed (ranked seventh), are actually making subpar or even zero profits (these and all subsequent rankings and online audience sizes are from Pew Research Center 2015, 11). For example, in 2014, Huffington Post's net profits (earnings before interest, taxes, depreciation, and amortization [EBITDA], the generally accepted measure) was zero, rising slightly in 2015 to a net profit of 6 percent (Berman 2015). This contrasts with newspaper companies' continued average of 8 to 15 percent, not to mention the much larger profit rates for cable TV news (Pew Research Center 2015, 33–34).

Digital media's sole reliance on online revenues underwrites staffs that are only skeletal and mostly low-paid, compared to those of digital media's print or television counterparts. For instance, the US Huffington Post with its 'monthly uniques' audience of one hundred million supports 260 full-time editorial workers, most of whom spend their time recycling content produced by other news organizations (Calderone 2016). In contrast, the *New York Times*, with its online audience of fifty-seven million and a subscribing audience of two million (one million each for print and online), maintains a full-time professional news staff of 1,300 (Pew Research Center 2014a; Doctor 2013), none of which is involved in aggregation.

Legacy media also tend to have the largest audiences online. In order, old lions like ABC (in partnership with Yahoo!), CNN, NBC, CBS, *USA Today*, *The New York Times* and Fox make up seven of the top ten news websites in the United States. Legacy media make up twenty-nine of the top fifty online news outlets by audience.

Even so, we can begin to discern some significant ways that this new digital media system differs from the relatively low-choice 'broadcast' system that preceded it (Prior 2007). For one thing, the Internet has broken down international barriers. Six of the top fifty US media are now British imports: Daily Mail (ranked tenth), BBC (fifteenth), Guardian (seventeenth), Telegraph Media Group (twenty-ninth), Mirror Online (fortieth), and Independent (forty-second). In addition to the BBC, non-commercial media are represented in the top fifty by the US NPR (nineteenth).

Beyond the top ten, which includes Huffington Post and BuzzFeed, online-only commercial news includes a range of outlets devoted to politics, sports, business and technology. Compared to the low-choice broadcast era of media, the fragmented digital system offers increased topical and often ideological diversity. There is also an increase in the diversity of forms and formats of journalistic practice.

Two US digital media outlets in particular are worth highlighting for their unique and in many ways admirable journalistic practices: Vox.com and ViceNews.com.

Instead of breaking news, Vox writers take complex issues—such as the Syrian conflict, Obama's health care plan, climate change, and so on—and provide in-depth explanations enlivened by graphs, questions and answers, and slide shows. So-called Vox card stacks provide serious but lively backgrounds for topics ranging from 'The 18 Best TV Shows Airing Right Now' (updated weekly) and 'Police Shootings and Brutality: 9 Things You Should Know' (both posted on January 4, 2016) to 'Bitcoin: Explained' (posted November 3, 2015) and 'The Basics of the US Immigration System' (posted August 4, 2015).

Vice, for its part, is unique for its highly personal, visually stunning, 'immersive' journalism. In its acclaimed series for HBO (also available for free on its website or YouTube channel), Vice documentaries provide rare glimpses of daily life in places like Syria, Ukraine, North Korea, Central African Republic and even ISIS's 'Islamic State' (the latter a recipient of a Peabody Award for journalistic excellence). As Vice correspondent Danny Gold explained at a recent New York event, the goal is to 'get out of the way' and act 'as a conduit' for documentary subjects to express their own views (Gold 2015). Vice is producing reporting no one else is and is reaching younger audiences (an average age of twenty-six) few if any other news outlets are attracting (Ip 2015).

Less admirably, Vice (along with BuzzFeed) is a pioneer in producing 'sponsored content' (also known as 'native advertising' or 'brand publishing'), which it actively courts through its slyly named marketing agency, 'Virtue'. For instance, a Vice website vertical 'The Creators Project', sponsored by 'founding partner Intel', often features news stories with engineers and artists using Intel products (Widdicombe 2013). The label 'founding partner'—rather than sponsor—is worth noting: It signals that today's corporate funders are not content with attaching their name to a program but rather seek to actively shape content to suit their interests. Vice cultivates an edgy, alternative vibe, but the commercial formula behind it is full-throttle capitalism. Its investors include Fox (James Murdoch now sits on the board), Time Warner Inc., Hearst, Disney, A&E Network and numerous venture capital firms.

In sum, the new digital outlets are a mixed bag. Even their virtues may just be part of a swiftly passing liminal moment, as intriguing experiments are tamed and captured by the usual commercial imperatives.

The conventional wisdom is that whatever commercial media cannot or will not do—local investigative reporting, sustained in-depth reporting on enduring social problems, and the like—will somehow be taken care of by philanthropy. Can non-profit journalism really fill the gap?

The Non-profit 'Alternative'

In 2011, a New York conference of foundation funders of media enterprises publicly declared that given the lack of adequate commercial and government support, foundations bore a major civic responsibility for finding solutions to the crisis of journalism (Grantmakers in Film + Electronic Media 2011). A 2014 survey of ninety-three non-profit news organizations found that about three-quarters received foundation funding, which usually made up the majority of their total revenues (Pew Research Center 2013, 19).

Leading non-profit news media clearly see their work as a form of public service. A Knight Foundation (2013) study of eighteen non-profits, representing local, state and national investigative organizations, found that they devoted from 34 percent to 85 percent of their budgets to editorial needs, compared to an average for commercial news operations of 12 percent to 16 percent. In another recent comprehensive survey of 172 non-profit news organizations founded since 1987, the Pew Research Center (2013, 6) showed that more than half focus on investigative reporting (21 percent), government (17 percent), or public and foreign affairs (13 percent).

Investigative journalism has received a significant boost from non-profit news organizations, most notably ProPublica (founded in 2008), which has won two Pulitzer Prizes, as well as the longer-established but expanding Center for Investigative Reporting (founded in 1977) and Center for Public Integrity (founded in 1989). In 2015, ProPublica's targets included the Red Cross ('How the Red Cross Raised Half a Billion Dollars for Haiti and Built Six Homes'), the New York Federal Reserve ('shining a bright light on the Fed's culture, a culture that seems to stifle dissent and has made regulators excessively cozy with the financial giants they are supposedly overseeing . . .') and hospitals' overly aggressive efforts to collect debts from working class families (ProPublica 2014). Despite such successes—all firmly within the realm of a modest, left-liberal reformist agenda—there are significant limits to the foundation 'solution' to the market failure of American commercial journalism.

Annual donations to news organizations are $150 million (Pew Research Center 2014c, 4, 20), a drop in the bucket compared to total US foundations' annual giving of $55 billion (Foundation Center 2014) or to the decreased $1.6 billion in annual commercial spending on editorial budgets since 2008 (Waldman 2011). Put another way, total revenues for all types of US news are about $60 billion; two-thirds of this amount still comes from advertising, and paying audiences account for most of the rest. Foundation contributions make up less than 1 percent of the total (Pew Research Center 2014b, 4).

The non-profit sector remains small however you measure it. The largest national non-profit news organizations, *Christian Science Monitor* and ProPublica, both have annual total budgets of around $10 million and employ eighty and fifty fulltime journalists, respectively (Lewis 2010). At the regional and local levels, the largest non-profits are *Texas Tribune* ($7 million budget, forty-two full-time journalists), followed at some distance by *MinnPost* ($1.6 million, seventeen journalists) and *Voice of San Diego* ($1.3 million, eleven journalists; Knight Foundation 2015, 6).

Most major foundations see themselves as providing not an antidote to the market, but rather short-term start-up support, with the expectation that non-profits will eventually achieve commercial 'sustainability' (Edmonds 2015). To achieve sustainability, elite non-profit media are encouraged to get their audiences to donate or subscribe. This formula moves non-profit media toward an increasingly exclusive mission, news by and for elites. *MinnPost* publisher Joel Kramer has been quoted as saying that monthly 'uniques' visiting his website are 'worse than worthless' and that he is really aiming for an elite, repeat readership of 'one-sixth of adults' (Edmonds 2013). Even at their most expansive, non-profit news sites measure their total audiences in the thousands rather than millions (Knight Foundation 2013, 14)—for example, 270,000 at *MinnPost* and 560,000 at *Texas Tribune*—while the overall average for non-profits is less than fifty thousand. Some outlets, such as ProPublica, also share their content with commercial outlets, expanding their reach but adding little or nothing to their bottom line.

Corporate sponsorships have also become a key element of non-profit sustainability. Non-profits that lack major foundation and business support, as the case of the *San Francisco Public Press* shows, are doomed to marginality.

San Francisco Public Press was launched in 2009 as a self-proclaimed 'Wall Street Journal for Working People'. The *Public Press* refuses advertising or corporate sponsorships as a matter of principle. Asked by *Columbia Journalism Review* in 2009 to write an 'imaginary retrospective' of the *Public Press* for the year 2014, Stoll (2009) 'recalled' the 'daily print launch in 2012' that 'allowed us to reach a whole new audience: the working class population in San Francisco'. Stoll continued: 'Low-income folk are of little value to the luxury-goods advertisers targeted by traditional papers, and the Internet doesn't ameliorate this because even in 2014, a third of that segment of the population has limited or no broadband Internet access at home'.

Stoll was right about the lack of advertiser interest in working-class audiences. Unfortunately, lacking adequate non-advertising support, his paper has not yet been able to find an effective way to reach them either. As of the end of 2015, the *Public Press* maintained a website (updated twice weekly) and sells a few thousand copies of a sixteen-page print magazine, priced at a dollar, four times a year. The *San Francisco Public Press* remains a lean operation, relying almost entirely on volunteer labour and an annual budget of less than $100,000 per year, half from local philanthropic organizations, 30 percent from individual donations, and the remaining 20 percent from print newspaper sales and other sources. The lesson is clear:

Non-profit media truly committed to overcoming market failure will struggle as long as major foundations are only looking for the next market solution.

Ultimately, it should also be remembered that foundation donations are not 'free' but rather constitute a redirection of public resources (dollars that could go to government if it were not for generous tax deductions) to non-transparent and unaccountable entities that have effectively assumed media policy responsibilities. As one leading media foundation official volunteered to me: 'We're not regulated. There's no accountability. I don't have to meet with anybody I don't want to meet with. None of us do. And I don't think that's a great system. So my responsibility is to be the best steward, but as a culture, as a democracy I don't actually think foundations are the best way of providing public goods' (Anonymous Foundation Official 2013).

Despite the language of civic duty that surrounds the foundation world like a golden haze, there are also often specific strings and metrics attached to grants. Foundations increasingly prefer funding specific projects to general operations. This obviously creates the possibility of a conflict of interest, or the appearance of such.

Far from being a source of independence, US 'public' media's reliance on philanthropy has created constant pressures to skew content to meet donors' demands. In recent years, a number of revelations have shown the depth of the problem: In 2012, PBS created a multi-part series on the US economy sponsored by Dow Chemical that closely tracked the company's major business interests; in 2013, it created a documentary about drones funded by Lockheed Martin, a drone manufacturer; and in 2014, it created a series entitled 'Pension Peril' about the problems caused by public employee pensions, funded by a billionaire investor's personal foundation that is, by its own account, pushing state and local legislators across the United States to 'stop promising a (retirement) benefit' to public employees (Sirota 2014). As PBS's ombudsman admitted, these scandals 'shine a light on . . . ethical compromises in funding arrangements and lack of real transparency for viewers caused, in part, by the complicated funding demands needed to support public broadcasting' (Getler 2014).

Conclusion: Creeping towards Oligarchy

The US hyper-commercial media system contrasts sharply with those of most other leading democracies, which anchor their own systems with a strong public media sector. A growing body of international comparative research has demonstrated that public media consistently provide more in-depth, ideologically diverse and critical news about public domestic and international affairs than commercial media (Benson 2013, 201–205) and play an important role in increasing citizen confidence and engagement in democratic institutions (Albæk et al. 2014).

What will be the end result of the American experiment in hyper-commercialism and philanthropy? Although there are some bright spots, a number of problems loom on the horizon for American news media: If current trends hold, full-time professional journalism will continue to be downsized. The tens of thousands of journalists being laid off at major legacy news organizations are not being replaced by the trickle of new jobs at digital and non-profit news organizations, not even close.

Digital-only commercial media are subject to even greater commercial pressures than their legacy predecessors were, as advertisers gain greater control over the editorial process via native advertising. The only escape from advertiser control seems to be increased reliance on reader contributions and subscriptions, which tend to favour high-income demographics and ultimately wall off most people from the promised civic and cultural benefits of the Internet.

As a whole, the US media system—increasingly privately held or foundation-funded—seems to be moving back toward the corrupt and agenda-driven media system that prevailed in the United States and most of Western Europe prior to World War II and that probably still is the global norm. In this kind of system, global oligarchs accept less than maximal profits in exchange for the obvious publicity—and silencing—power of the media. This doesn't mean there won't be quality journalism anymore, but are clearly limits. As economic power becomes increasingly concentrated, these limits will degrade the quality of democratic life. Any media reform worthy of the name will need to address these new challenges.

References

Albæk, E., A. V. Dalen, N. Jebril, and C. H. De Vreese. 2014. *Political Journalism in Comparative Perspective*. New York: Cambridge University Press.

Anonymous Foundation Official. 2013. Interview with author, March.

Baker, C. E. 2002. *Media, Markets, and Democracy*. New York: Cambridge University Press.

Benson, R., and M. Powers. 2011. *Public Media and Political Independence*. Washington, DC: Free Press.

Benson, R. 2013. *Shaping Immigration News: A French-American Comparison*. New York: Cambridge University Press.

Berman, D. K. 2015. "Is Huffington Post Worth $1 Billion?" *The Wall Street Journal*, June 12. http://www.wsj.com/articles/is-huffington-post-worth-1 -billion-1434101405.

Calderone, M. 2016. "The Huffington Post Management Voluntarily Recognizes Employee Unions." *The Huffington Post*, January 14. http://www.huffingtonpost .com/entry/huffington-post-union_us_5697d72be4b0b4eb759d79fc.

Doctor, K. 2013. "The Newsonomics of Pulitzers, Paywalls, and Investing in the Newsroom." *NiemanLab*, April 18. http://www.niemanlab.org/2013/04/ the-newsonomics-of-pulitzers-paywalls-and-investing-in-the-newsroom/.

Downie, L., Jr., and M. Schudson. 2009. "The Reconstruction of American Journalism." *Columbia Journalism Review* 19 (November/December). http:// www.cjr.org/reconstruction/the_reconstruction_of_american.php.

Edmonds, R. 2013. "Non-profit Sites Are Proving to Be Healthy but Slow to Scale." Poynter, September 26. http://www.poynter.org/news/mediawire/ 224396/nonprofit-journalism-sites-are-proving-to-be-healthy-but-slow -to-scale/.

Edmonds, R. 2015. "Knight Foundation Finds Nonprofit Sites' Revenue Rising but Sustainability Elusive." Poynter, April 8. http://www.poynter.org/news/ mediawire/332021/knight-foundation-finds-nonprofit-sites-revenue-rising-but- sustainability-elusive/.

Enda, J. 2010. "Retreating from the World." *American Journalism Review* (Winter), 14–29.

Foundation Center. 2014. *Key Facts on US Foundations*. http://foundation center.org/gainknowledge/research/keyfacts2014/pdfs/Key_Facts_on_US_ Foundations_2014.pdf.

Getler, M. 2014. "Tensions over Pensions." *PBS Ombudsman*, February 14. http://www.pbs.org/ombudsman/2014/02/tensions_over_pensions_1.html.

Gold, D. 2015. Author's notes on remarks at New York Center for Communication Event for Vice Media, New York, November 23.

Grantmakers in Film + Electronic Media. 2011. Author's fieldnotes from Media + Technology Funding Outlook: The State and Future of the Field conference, New York, June 16.

Ip, C. 2015. "The Cult of Vice." *Columbia Journalism Review* (July/August). http://www.cjr.org/analysis/the_cult_of_vice.php.

Knight Foundation. 2013. "Finding a Foothold: How Nonprofit News Ventures Seek Sustainability." Knight Foundation, October 29. http://knightfoundation .org/publications/finding-foothold.

Knight Foundation. 2015. "Gaining Ground: How Nonprofit News Ventures Seek Sustainability." Knight Foundation, April 8. http://knightfoundation.org/ publications/gaining-ground-how-nonprofit-news-ventures-seek-su.

Lewis, C. 2010. "New Journalism Ecosystem Thrives." Investigative Reporting Workshop: American University School of Communication, October 29. http:// investigativereportingworkshop.org/ecosystem/#viewall.

Meyer, P. 2006. *The Vanishing Newspaper*. Columbia: University of Missouri Press.

Mitchell, D. 2012. "Profits Aren't the Only Consideration for Newspapers." *Fortune*, June 7. http://fortune.com/2012/06/07/profits-arent-the-only -consideration-for-newspapers/.

O'Shea, J. 2011. *The Deal from Hell: How Moguls and Wall Street Plundered Great American Newspapers*. New York: Public Affairs.

Pew Research Center. 2013. "Nonprofit Journalism: A Growing but Fragile Part of the U.S. News System," June 10. http://www.journalism.org/files/legacy/ Nonprofit%20News%20Study.pdf.

Pew Research Center. 2014a. "The Growth in Digital Reporting: What It Means for Journalism and News Consumers." Pew Research Center, March 26. http:// www.journalism.org/2014/03/26/the-growth-in-digital-reporting/.

Pew Research Center. 2014b. "State of the News Media 2014: Overview." http:// www.journalism.org/2014/03/26/state-of-the-news-media-2014-overview/.

Pew Research Center. 2014c. "The Revenue Picture for American Journalism, and How It Is Changing." Pew Research Center, March 26. http://www .journalism.org/2014/03/26/the-revenue-picture-for-american-journalism -and-how-it-is-changing/.

Pew Research Center. 2015. "State of the News Media 2015," April 29. http:// www.journalism.org/files/2015/04/FINAL-STATE-OF-THE-NEWS-MEDIA.pdf.

Prior, M. 2007. *Post-Broadcast News*. New York: Cambridge University Press.

ProPublica. 2014. "Annual Report: 'No Story Too Big, No Subject Too Powerful.'" http://www.propublica.org/about/.

Sirota, D. 2014. "The Wolf of Sesame Street: Revealing the Secret Corruption inside PBS's News Division." PandoDaily, February 12. https://pando.com/2014/02/12/the-wolf-of-sesame-street-revealing-the-secret-corruption-inside-pbss-news-division/.

Stoll, M. 2009. "No Profit, No Problem: How a New City Daily (on Newsprint!) Rolled." *Columbia Journalism Review* (March/April). http://www.cjr.org/feature/no_profit_no_problem_1.php?page=all.

Waldman, S. 2011. *The Information Needs of Communities*. Washington, DC: Federal Communications Commission.

Walton, M. 2010. "Investigative Shortfall." *American Journalism Review* (Fall), 19–30.

WAN (World Association of Newspapers). 2007. *World Press Trends*. Paris: World Association of Newspapers.

Widdicombe, L. 2013. "The Bad-Boy Brand." *The New Yorker*, April 8.

II

··

Public Knowledge in Britain

Part II looks at other forms of public knowledge in Britain and their erosion since 2010. Across a variety of sectors, the coalition and then Conservative governments have applied a mix of severe cuts, covert privatization measures and market-inspired public sector reorganisations. In each case, both the transition and its wider impacts have been obscured, with public debate squeezed, official statistics buried and government and corporate spin liberally disseminated. In the case of legal aid and libraries, the pathways and outcomes are simple: severe cuts, with the mass of ordinary citizens being deprived of legal and other forms of public knowledge. In education, the story is more complex. Large parts of the higher education system have already been privatized. The academisation of schools suggests, like the recent restructuring of the NHS, that full-scale marketization of education may not be far away. Ironically, marketisation in this case does not equal greater individual and organisational choice and autonomy; instead, it seems to be leading to more centralised government control.

Chapter 7 asks: What exactly is happening to our school system since post-2010 administrations began forcing through a mixture of academisation and centralisation? What does it mean for children and teachers, and where is it all leading? Ken Jones sketches out the bigger picture, one in which education is increasingly driven by a conflicting mixture of private, market-led bodies and state-set targets and audits, with prior educational ideals dropping down the priority order.

Next, in chapter 8, Andrew McGettigan explores the economic and financial logic through which the UK Treasury has justified transformations in the funding and financing of higher education (HE) in the UK. Following the tripling of university fees and the botched introduction of an unsustainable loan system, the government has made further attempts to make HE 'a market'. The Treasury in particular looks at education as a form of 'human capital' and wants to redirect student and HE institutional choices towards a logic of investment and future returns.

One of the most controversial sets of cuts imposed by the coalition government was to legal aid provision and related legal services. In chapter 9, Roger Smith asks: Quite apart from the social consequences of this move, what are the larger economic outcomes of it? He makes the case that a clear discussion of this question has been obstructed by noise from all sides, but dominated especially by official sources. In the process, the true direct and indirect costs, both financial and social, are being obscured. Equally concerning, the great gains of the 'welfare rights' movement, as they related to the justice system, are now being cast out altogether.

In chapter 10, Ian Anstice offers an overview of how local library services across the United Kingdom have been affected by cuts. As he explains, although only 10 percent have been axed since 2010, the hidden real-terms cuts go far deeper. Services and provisions offered have been drastically reduced and reshaped in a number of ways that only partially paper over what is happening. As with other public institutions, such cuts, tacitly supported by the coalition and Conservative governments, have undermined the very principles upon which local libraries were built.

7

The Autonomous School, the Strong State, the Problems of Education

Ken Jones

Since its election victory, the Conservative party has wasted no time in getting on with its education programme—essentially an acceleration and extension of policies developed by the previous coalition government. Its centrepiece is the attempt to convert most English schools into academies—institutions that are publicly financed but are not accountable to any elected body, other than central government itself.[1]

In some ways, this looks like a programme of marketization: the creation of a landscape buzzing with the activity of private companies, filled with autonomous schools managed by leaders incentivised to innovate and to discover through experiment 'what works' and what can drive standards ever higher. However, this is not the whole picture. Since the Education Reform Act of 1988, the measures of marketization introduced into English schooling have been intertwined with the strengthening of the powers of central government. Making sense of this private-public amalgam—sketching its trajectory and anticipating its problems—is both a complex analytical task and a worthwhile political project. It brings into view the outlines of a dynamic and unstable system, which has had powerful effects on knowledge production and educational work—effects that merit both exploration and challenge.

Towards Academisation

There are around twenty-two thousand state schools in England—about seventeen thousand primaries and 3,200 secondaries. There are a diminishing number of nursery schools—around five hundred—and nearly one thousand special schools. Since 2010, governments have been trying to persuade and in some cases compel schools to become academies. The result of this recruitment drive, which is supported by a special unit of the Department for Education (DfE), is that as of June 2015, there are 4,676 academies of all types open across England (House of Commons Library 2015). Sixty-one percent of secondary schools are academies, as are 14 percent of primaries (DfE 2015a). A school becomes an academy by either conversion or sponsorship. *Conversion* is a process through which the existing governing body takes over from an elected local authority control over admissions, performance, assets and finances. By this means, billions of pounds of public wealth have been transferred into private hands. With *sponsorship*, the same ends are achieved through the intervention of an outside agency, approved by the DfE to take over an 'underperforming' school. Sponsors can include other educational institutions, as well as 'businesses and entrepreneurs, educational foundations, charities and philanthropists and faith communities' (DfE 2015b).

In this variegated landscape—in which the old forms of coordination and governance, exercised through local authorities

and local representation in governing bodies, are in decline—
new forms arise. The multi-academy chain—a group of academies with a single sponsor—is one such form. Under the
coalition government, the number of chains increased, as did
the number of schools that they controlled. In 2010, Absolute
Return for Kids (ARK) managed eight schools; by the end of
2014, the number had risen to thirty-one; the Harris Federation
managed nine in 2010 and by 2014 controlled twenty-seven;
United Learning, linked to the Church of England, increased
from thirteen to forty-one. In June 2014, the DfE listed 192
chains, some running more than fifty schools, the majority only
three or four (Hutchings, Francis and Kirby 2015).

The influence of these organisations has spilled over from
school management to wider fields of policy. ARK, for instance—
closely involved with the financial sector from which it draws
much of its funding—has become involved in professional development, teacher training, curriculum and learning strategies
development. In the process, it has brought 'new practices and
methods from the business sector to bear upon the education
problems it addressed' and become an 'active agent of education reform' (Junemann and Ball 2013). The DfE is keen that this
process of agency should be extended and works to achieve the
appointment of 'exceptional business leaders to the boards of
multi-academy trusts' (Morgan 2015). As the influence of business leaders grows, the role of parents and teachers in governing bodies will be reduced.

Government as Co-ordinator

Many aspects of state schooling are thus shaped by private sector influence, and there is profit to be made in many places, from

the provision of supply teachers to the maintenance of buildings to consultancy, research and policy advice. But it would be a mistake to see this proliferation of activity as a sign that the future of schooling will be organised along full market lines, with change being driven by competition among private educational entities seeking to maximise their market share. From the supplier's standpoint, it is difficult to make a consistent profit from a business in which staff costs are so high as a percentage of total expenditure; from the regulator's standpoint, it is difficult to guarantee standards across the diversity of a fully marketised system. Thus, although policy has favoured private sector involvement in schooling, it has not adopted a voucher-based or 'user pays' approach. That decisive step towards marketisation is one that governments shrink away from taking.

The emphasis of policy has thus fallen elsewhere. Both New Labour and Conservative administrations have held on tightly to the role that government was allocated in 1988, a role of steering the system so that it follows procedures and pursues goals that are ever more closely specified by a central authority. It is not to parental demand that the system answers but to the central state—a form of accountability that is stronger now than ever before.

Steering is based on a collection of data about school performance, focused on levels of success in tests and exams. The widely publicised league tables provide one way of presenting the data. Another, more powerful instrument is the Ofsted Data Dashboard, which 'provides a snapshot of performance in a school' to which Ofsted inspectors will refer 'to compare the performance of a school with others with which it is deemed to be comparable' (Ofsted, n.d.). Likewise, another Ofsted site, Raise Online, provides teachers with an 'interactive analysis of school and pupil performance data', intended as a resource for school improvement (RaiseOnline, n.d.). The appeal to the authority of data also underlies the mechanisms that the government proposes for further academisation. *Coasting schools*—those destined for forced academisation—are defined by their failure to meet targets of pupil attainment and pupil progress (Dickens 2015).

In short, schooling is at many levels 'governed by data', subject to what Jenny Ozga calls *highly centralised system steering* (Ozga 2009). Decisions over such matters as how pupils should be grouped, how teachers should be managed and who should own an academy (Rosen 2014) are arrived at and justified with reference to 'what the data tells us'. However, although policymakers continue to believe in the truth of data, the processes through which it is collected and reported on are elsewhere called into question. 'It's hard to put numbers on to knowledge', writes the blogger Jack Marwood, 'but that hasn't stopped people trying to do just that', and since the National Curriculum was introduced in 1988, children have been assessed as being at different levels based on what knowledge, skills and understanding various experts have said they should have. Once possessed of such 'numbers', Marwood goes on, government agencies have processed them in statistically disreputable ways—treating schools with very different populations as if they are comparable (Marwood 2014).

Effects

Recent research by Merryn Hutchings reports the effects of this data-driven system on pupils. Schools have to maximise their scores, in the narrow range of subjects that policy prescribes.

Teachers spoke to Hutchings of a primary timetable 'dominated by Maths and English lessons, plus daily spelling/reading/mental maths'; year six pupils in one primary school worked on no subjects other than maths and English in the months between their return to school in September and their SATs tests the following May. Secondary teachers made similar comments: 'Ultimately, if you are going to put in an accountability system . . . you're going to have other aspects that are not accounted for, and I'm talking holistic development of a child' (Hutchings 2015, 18). The much-discussed problems of stress and unhappiness among young people stem in important part from the priorities of the school system.

Teachers, operationally central to this system, are themselves under great pressure. Whatever they demand of children is demanded of them first. Hutchings' report is full of their testimonies: 'There is a real sense of fear and we are driven by SLT [the senior leadership team] to work harder and harder and push the pupils harder and harder'; 'I am totally exhausted all the time. I work 60–70 hours a week just to keep up with what I am expected to do . . . Many teachers in my workplace are feeling permanently stressed and demoralised. More of us are looking to leave as more and more workload is being given with no regard to its impact on teachers or the children' (Hutchings 2015, 32).

For governments, the capacity of management to exert pressure on teachers to improve test scores is central to school improvement. The Conservative government, like every other government this century, has expanded this capacity, with an armoury of incentives and punitive resources. Under the coalition, the national pay system was dismantled, and managements were given greater discretion over pay levels. All pay progression is now linked to performance, in a salary system based on individualised decision. Likewise, there are no effective limits to the working day. Teaching remains one of the most strongly unionised occupations, and unions have in some schools been able to hold in check the demands of 'senior leadership teams'. However, the overall shift in power is unmistakeable: away from a professionalism centred on notions of expertise and discretion and towards a conception of teachers' work based on the effective implementation of procedures determined by management.

Knowledge

In the current school system, questions of educational value tend to be non-negotiable. Value is measured in test results, which provide the data for arguments about the respective effectiveness of different types of school, different styles of teaching and so on. The initial training and later professional development of teachers is discussed from a similar standpoint. This is one reason that universities, which historically have been settings in which education has been discussed in wider terms and the meaning of 'effectiveness' has been up for debate, are being pushed out of a central role in teacher education. Increasingly, what counts as knowledge is supplied from other sources. The Education Endowment Foundation, funded partly by government and partly by a private trust, is dedicated to 'extending the evidence base on what works' and making it available to teachers (Education Endowment Foundation, n.d.). It compiles reviews of largely quantitative research into strategies for improving attainment and rates them for effectiveness. Other organisations—the Teacher Development Trust, the emergent

College of Teaching, local Teaching Schools Alliances—convey a similar message: Teachers should 'draw upon (and contribute to) readily-available sources of leading evidence-based approaches, confidently engaging with high quality research and evaluation' (Teacher Development Trust, n.d.).

Tensions

The growing involvement of the private sector and the strengthening of the central apparatus of government are intertwined developments in a coherent reshaping of the governance of English schooling. The logic of the 'state form' of English schooling has unfolded over nearly thirty years and now reached a new level of intensity. The lineaments of an early system—based on control of schools by local authorities, with strong teacher influence over curriculum and pedagogy—can no longer be discerned. The powers of the central apparatus to shape educational process through the identification, collection and management of data are stronger than at any point since 1988. Equally unrestricted is the capacity of the school leaderships of autonomised schools to micromanage the work of teachers.

Yet the system that has been shaped by these changes exacerbates rather than resolves long-standing problems of education. Most evidently, it imposes a set of constraints that prevent schools from innovating at any level of depth. The curriculum enforced through tests and exam syllabuses is narrow and in some subject areas flagrantly regressive; it sets aside, for instance, most of what researchers know about language and learning, in favour of a 'naming of parts' approach focused on grammatical understandings that were popular early in the previous century (Rosen 2013). An anachronism even at the time of its birth, it is hard to see this codification of knowledge surviving for long.

The rigidities of the curriculum are matched by other features of the system that may well prove equally problematic. Despite the regulatory programme of government, the outcomes of schooling differ considerably among academy chains, and the gap between the best and the worst is increasing (Hutchings, Francis and Kirby 2015). The harsh discipline inflicted on teachers may produce compliance in the short term, but as a means of encouraging engagement in educational improvement it will be ineffective. Likewise, the incessant pressure on students, especially in the upper years of schooling, will not continue to produce generations of diligent exam-takers. Education and training up to the age of eighteen have become compulsory precisely at the moment when the promise that educational success will be rewarded with career security has plainly become impossible to deliver. If it is reasonable to think that the precarity of social life in the long transition between 'youth' and 'adulthood' will lead to explosive moments of protest, then it will equally be unsurprising if such moments are not also experienced by sixteen year olds. In the school, as elsewhere, the very inventiveness of neoliberalism and its tendency to dissolve the solidities of an established system may now have created tensions that threaten its existence.

Note

1. For a concise (ten-page) explanation of the different types of school in the English system, see New Schools Network (2015).

References

DfE (Department for Education). 2015a. "Schools, Pupils and Their Characteristics: January 2015." https://www.gov.uk/government/uploads/system/uploads/attachment_data/file/433680/SFR16_2015_Main_Text.pdf.

DfE (Department for Education). 2015b. "Sponsor an Academy: Guidance." https://www.gov.uk/sponsor-an-academy.

Dickens, J. 2015. "Coasting School Definition Revealed by Nicky Morgan." *Schools Week*, June 30. http://schoolsweek.co.uk/coasting-school-definition-revealed-by-nicky-morgan/.

Education Endowment Foundation. n.d. "Our Approach to Evaluation." https://educationendowmentfoundation.org.uk/.

House of Commons Library. 2015. Briefing Paper "Education and Adoption Bill 2014/15." June 17, 2015. http://researchbriefings.files.parliament.uk/documents/CBP-7232/CBP-7232.pdf.

Hutchings, M. 2015. *Exam Factories? The Effect of Accountability Measures on Children and Young People.* London: National Union of Teachers.

Hutchings, M., B. Francis, and P. Kirby. 2015. "Chain Effects 2015: The Impact of Academy Chains on Low-Income Students." http://www.suttontrust.com/wp-content/uploads/2015/07/Chain-Effects-2015.pdf.

Junemann, C. and Ball, B. 2013. "ARK and the Revolution of State Education in England." *Education Inquiry* 4 (3): 423–441.

Marwood, J. 2014. "RAISEonline Is Contemptible Rubbish." Icing on the Cake, March 17. http://icingonthecakeblog.weebly.com/blog/raiseonline-is-contemptible-rubbish.

Morgan, N. 2015. Secretary of State for Education, speech to the National Governors Association, Manchester, June 27.

New Schools Network. 2015. "Comparison of Different Types of School: A Guide to Schools in England." http://www.newschoolsnetwork.org/sites/default/files/Comparison%20of%20school%20types.pdf.

Ofsted. n.d. "Ofsted Data Dashboard" http://dashboard.ofsted.gov.uk/index.php.

Ozga, J. 2009. "Governing Education through Data in England: From Regulation to Self-Evaluation." *Journal of Education Policy* 24 (2): 149–162.

RaiseOnline. n.d. https://www.raiseonline.org/login.aspx?ReturnUrl=%2f.

Rosen, M. 2013. "Lies about Spelling, Punctuation, Grammar Test." Michael Rosen, April 6. http://michaelrosenblog.blogspot.co.uk/2013/04/lies-about -spellingpunctuationgrammar.html.

Rosen, M. 2014. "Who Owns Academies? Have We Been Robbed?" Michael Rosen, March 4. http://michaelrosenblog.blogspot.co.uk/2014/03/who-owns -academies-have-we-been-robbed.html.

Teacher Development Trust. n.d. "Our Mission." http://tdtrust.org/about/ mission/.

8

The Treasury View of Higher Education:
Variable Human Capital Investment

Andrew McGettigan

If we are concerned about public knowledge and the political economy of its production, then we need to attend to the manner in which the funding of undergraduate study in England was transformed in 2012. Higher tuition fees were licensed by government at publicly funded institutions so that the latter could use fee income to cover large cuts to the direct public funding of tuition. Grants to universities and colleges were cut by roughly £3 billion per year, and students pursuing 'classroom' subjects, such as politics and economics, are now solely funded by fee income. At the same time, loans to students were extended so that a maximum of £9,000 per year could be borrowed to cover these fees.[1]

This generalised fee-loan regime is more than a temporary austerity measure. Its architect, David Willetts, the former Minister for Universities and Science, wrote in 2013 that 'unleashing the forces of consumerism is the best single way we've got of restoring high academic standards' (Willetts 2013). Flagging up the course costs to students is meant to make them think more carefully about their university choices and make them demand more when they arrive to study.

However, that is only the first step in the transition. The focus of policy has been the transformation of higher education into the private good of training and the positional good of opportunity, where the returns on both are higher earnings. Initiation into the production and dissemination of public knowledge does not appear to be a concern of current policy.

Such an anti-vision of higher education—letting the market determine what should be offered—unfortunately meshes with a stratified higher education sector that mirrors an increasingly unequal society. This chapter outlines the next phase of English higher education policy, which will exacerbate the erosion of public knowledge from the institutions traditionally most associated with it.

The coalition government quietly put in place a series of measures designed to support a new performance metric: repayment of loans by course and institution. This could become the one metric to dominate all others and will be theorised under the rubric of 'human capital investment'.

The Small Business, Enterprise and Employment Act received Royal Assent at the end of March 2015. Part 6 of the Act is titled 'Education Evaluation' (UK Government 2015a). It proposed amendments to existing legislation to allow the co-ordination of data collected by the Higher Education Statistics Agency and HM Revenue & Customs. The Department for Business, Innovation & Skills (BIS) provided a gloss on the measures (UK Government 2015b). Potential applicants to colleges and universities will benefit in the future from information about the 'employability and earnings' of each institution's alumni and alumnae: 'The measures will enable information on earnings and employability to be evaluated more effectively which will inform student choice. This data, presented in context, will distinguish universities that are delivering durable labour market outcomes and a strong enterprise ethos for their students' (UK Government 2015b, 3).

Applicants could inform themselves about the future earnings of those who followed a particular course and choose where to study accordingly. In its 2015 manifesto, the Conservative party pledged to 'require more data to be openly available to potential students so that they can make decisions informed by the career paths of past graduates' (Conservatives 2015, 35).

The Act was a move in a new phase of tertiary education policy. In 2012, a new question had been added to the annual Labour Force Survey to allow 'analysis of long-run earnings outcomes from specific institutions'. In July 2014, Lord Young's report for government, *Enterprise for All*, had recommended that each course at each institution should have to publish a Future Earnings and Employment Record 'so that students can assess the full costs and likely benefits of specific courses at specific institutions'. One section of the report was helpfully titled 'What FEER Can Do' (BIS/PMO 2014). In October 2013, David Willetts expressed his enthusiasm for a new research project funded by the Nuffield Foundation:'Professor Neil Shephard of Harvard University and Professor Anna Vignoles of Cambridge University are currently merging a wealth of data from the Student Loans Company and HM Revenue and Customs which should deliver a significant improvement in the current data on labour market outcomes of *similar courses at different institutions*' (Willetts 2013, 19; my emphasis).

The research project cited here is titled 'Estimating Human Capital of Graduates', and published its initial findings in 2016

(Britton et al. 2016). It sought to assess how the future earnings of 'similar students' vary 'by institution type and subject'. The project website captures this aspiration and its policy implications: 'If different degrees from different institutions result in very different levels of earnings for students with similar pre-university qualifications and from similar socio-economic backgrounds, then this might affect both student choice and policies designed to increase participation and improve social mobility'.[2] That paragraph presents the two angles to this debate: it is not just applicants who want to know what their monetary return on further study might be. Moving beyond consumer choice, the government as lender is becoming increasingly concerned by the size of the subsidy built in to the student loan scheme as the latter is buffeted by recession, low bank base rates, a troubling graduate labour market and earlier mistakes in the modelling of future repayments.

In England, annual student loan issues are now over £10 billion and are set to continue climbing to about £14 billion by 2018/19. Repayments in 2014 languished at around £1.5 billion. At the time, BIS reckoned it would only get back the equivalent of 55 percent of the £10 billion amount issued each year. 45 percent would therefore be lost as non-repayment. When the new higher maximum tuition fee was voted through in December 2010, it had been assumed that the relevant repayment figure would be 70 percent. Each percentage point of variance is the equivalent of £100 million in lost value (1 percent of £10 billion). Therefore, a drop of fifteen percentage points meant that BIS was £1.5 billion worse off than expected on a single year's outlay.

There are various methods open to government to manage such shortfalls, but the Treasury is loath to abandon the new funding regime, because a low return on a loan is still better than money spent on grants, money that is spent and does not come back in the form of repayments. What the Treasury wants is information on good institutions.

The 2011 Higher Education white paper presented undergraduate degrees as human capital investments that *benefit* private individuals insofar as the degrees enable those individuals to boost their future earnings. Universities and colleges are then to be judged on how well they provide training that does indeed boost earnings profiles. Such 'value add' would displace current statistical concoctions based on prior attainment and final degree classification. The key device is loans: loans go out into the world, and the manner in which they are repaid generates information. Graduates then become the bearers of the units of account by which HE performance is set into a system of accountability: 'What level of repayments is this graduate of this course likely to produce over the next 35 years?'

As Willetts previously argued in 2012, the figure for non-repayment of loans in the departmental accounts—that 45 percent—is an aggregate for a sector comprising over one hundred higher education institutions, three hundred further education colleges offering HE, and one hundred private providers 'designated' as eligible for student support. Thus the overall non-repayment figure masks variation in performance by subject (e.g., medicine and law graduates repay more), institution and sex. Willetts has indicated enthusiasm for robust disaggregation of the figures:'I expect that, in the future, as the data accrue, the policy debate will be about the [non-repayment rate] for individual institutions . . . *the actual Exchequer risk from lending to students at specific universities*' (Willetts 2011; my emphasis).

It is this question of risk that returns us to what is the ur-text for English higher education policy: Milton Friedman's 1955 essay, 'The Role for Government in Education' (Friedman 1955). In the second half of that text, Friedman discusses higher education—in particular, professional and vocational education— and offers his understanding of human capital: '[Education is] a form of investment in human capital precisely analogous to investment in machinery, buildings, or other forms of non-human capital. Its function is to raise the economic *productivity* of the human being. If it does so, the individual is rewarded in a free enterprise society by receiving a higher return for his services' (Friedman 1955).

There is a role for government in providing loans to individuals for such study, because capital market imperfections render such loans expensive or impossible to secure without collateral.[3] 'Existing imperfections in the capital market tend to restrict the more expensive vocational and professional training to individuals whose parents or benefactors can finance the training required. They make such individuals a 'non-competing' group *sheltered from competition by the unavailability of the necessary capital to many individuals*, among whom must be large numbers with equal ability. The result is to perpetuate inequalities in wealth and status' (Friedman 1955; my emphasis).

The problem from a national perspective is therefore 'underinvestment' and inequity (a lack of social mobility). Government intervention is justified if there are too few graduates or if graduates only come from the privileged classes. Friedman (1955) sketches a precursor to the income-contingent repayment loan (ICR loan) that underpins English tuition fee policy. He proposes that the government 'buy a share in an individual's earning prospects'—that is, that the government 'advances [the student] the funds needed to finance his training on condition that he agree to pay the lender a specified fraction of his future earnings [sic]'.

As England has transitioned towards Friedman's idea over the last twenty years (add the current policy to write off outstanding balances thirty-one years after graduation, and you have ICR loans), we have reached a hybrid loan-voucher scheme with a large subsidy provided by government (that 45 percent of estimated non-repayment again). Friedman was explicit: a loan scheme should be self-financing, and individuals should 'bear the costs of investing in themselves'. That said, he goes on to argue that money should follow the individual in either form, as loan or voucher, rather than being paid to institutions: 'The subsidisation of institutions rather than of people has led to an indiscriminate subsidization of whatever activities it is appropriate for such institutions to undertake, rather than of activities it is appropriate for the state to subsidise. The problem is not primarily that we are spending too little money . . . but that we are getting so little per dollar spent' (Friedman 1955).

And here is the rub. The growing and unexpectedly large subsidy built into the current iteration of the fee loan regime points to that same problem: the government is not getting the maximum from borrowers or from universities (which are using tuition fees to subsidise other activities, like research). One might blame universities that set fees for classroom subjects at the same rate as lab-based subjects (that blanket £9,000 per annum), or loan funding offered for subjects that do nothing to boost graduate productivity. Either way, it points to the issue of mis-investment rather than underinvestment. Indeed, given the statistics on graduates filling posts that do not require graduate qualifications, from the human capital theory perspective one might even use the language of *overinvestment in HE*. It is not clear to many whether the problems of the graduate labour market are recessionary, structural, secular or a combination of all three.[4]

Belief in the generic value of a degree and its centrality to the neo-endogenous growth theory of the nineties is on the wane. There is now a cross-party consensus growing around the need to boost tech skills, through degree apprenticeships and Labour's idea of a new *dual track* system. The latter term was chosen to deflect any suggestion of a return to the pre-1993 binary system of HE, but in March 2015, Vince Cable went so far as to lament the abolition of polytechnics at an Association of Colleges event.

Human capital theory addresses this question—about the risk of undesired subsidy and mis-investment—through Gary Becker's redefinition of *moral hazard*: 'Children can default on the market debt contracted for them by working less energetically or by entering occupations with lower earnings and higher psychic income' (Becker 1991, 247).

In a different register, ministers have been looking back to Lionel Robbins's 1963 higher education report for an inspiring slogan that launched a key phase of expansion: 'Higher education should be offered to anyone who can benefit'. What needs underscoring is that the definition of *benefit* is being transformed by what I called *financialisation* in *The Great University Gamble* (McGettigan 2013). Benefit now walks forward redefined in monetary terms as *creditworthiness*—of institutions and individuals. To ventriloquise: 'If this student with these qualifications from this background takes this course, how much should we lend them towards fees? Is this an institution that provides training that increases graduate earnings?'

In September 2012, Willetts outlined the dream: 'Imagine that in the future we discover that the RAB charge [non-repayment rate] for a Bristol graduate was 10 per cent. Maybe some other university . . . we are only going to get 60 per cent back. Going beyond that it becomes an interesting question, to what extent you can incentivise universities to lower their own RAB charges' (Willetts 2012). On the down side, the easiest way for universities to 'lower their own non-repayment rates' is to reduce fees or alter the balance of subjects and places they offer. For the government as lender, removing access to loans—'de-designation'—would represent a significant sanction against institutions, though the threat of any withdrawal will be stronger than the execution.

In the first instance, however, the evaluation data sought by that series of measures I outlined earlier only needs to be good enough to justify two tiers of maximum fees: a normal maximum and a higher one for high-cost subjects at 'successful' institutions. To mimic the vice-chancellors at the elite end of things: 'We are losing money on our high-cost subjects, but our graduates are good for higher borrowing, so give us dispensation to set a tuition fee above the current maximum.' Friedman rejected the idea of a flat offer to all applicants: '[The repayment demanded] should in principle vary from individual to individual in accordance with any differences in expected earning capacity that can be predicted in advance—the problem is similar to that of varying life insurance premia among groups that have different life expectancy' (Friedman 1955).

Variance of this kind would have an additional 'benefit' from the free market perspective of the Treasury: so long as there is a significant subsidy beneath the lending, then the tuition fee is prevented from fulfilling the signalling function neoclassically associated with price.[5] The headline fee does not provide this key function, because you cannot tell how much you are actually likely to repay after graduating. This means that students are prone to 'moral hazard' by making choices other than for reasons of productive investment. (Unlike Friedman's idea of a voucher, the loan subsidy received by any given individual is unpredictable and uncertain.)

If price is to be the single best indicator of quality, reflect future cost and dissuade mis-investment, then the subsidy must be eroded as much as possible. That's the neoclassical logic. The first step here is the likely freezing of the repayment threshold for the latest loans at £21,000 after 2016. As graduate earnings rise in the following years, 'fiscal drag' would generate more repayments and address immediate concerns about the 'sustainability' and 'generosity' of repayment terms. Graduates would however be paying more than they would have anticipated in 2012.

What I have outlined here, the coming wave of 'education evaluation', threatens to supplant traditional understandings of universities as communities advancing public knowledge. Current regulations governing the awarding of degrees aver that standards are maintained and safeguarded only by the critical activity of the academic community within an institution. It will be harder and harder to recall that fact.

As a conclusion, it should be recognised that human capital theory presents itself as a progressive theory in support of social mobility. Human capital investments 'dominate' (in the language of economics) ability and would be the preserve of the wealthy without state intervention. What is crucial then is access to the professions—hence the more recent concern with postgraduate loans. New data on the performance of institutions would then help those making investment decisions in a market currently saturated with proxy information and hundreds of rival institutions.

The risk is that academics seeking to resist this further privatisation of knowledge will be cast as those with vested interests seeking to protect an old, inadequate system lacking in transparency. We will end up on the wrong side of the argument. The difficulty: How do we articulate what is threatened? How do we defend forms of knowledge that are not subordinate to private returns? Academic freedom and autonomy now face a more pressing, insidious, financialised threat than the traditional bugbear of direct political interference. But all this may prove too abstract for effective resistance.

I have no glib solution to which you might sign up. But when hard times find us, criticism must strike for the root: in this case, undergraduate study as a stratified, unequal, positional good dominating future opportunities and outcomes. What might find broader public support is a vision of higher education institutions that are civic and open to lifelong participation, instead of places beholden to the three-year, full-time degree leveraged on loans and aiming to cream off 'talent'.

What is needed is a recasting of the very structure of undergraduate provision, one in tune with concerted interventions in economic, industrial and labour market policy. This would upset traditional notions of higher education, but it is not clear that they were ever adequate to the mass, not to say universal, public knowledge envisaged, for example, by Raymond Williams' 'third revolution': 'We speak of a cultural revolution, and we must certainly see the aspiration to extend the active process of learning, with the skills of literacy and other advanced communication, to all people rather than to limited groups, as comparable in importance to the growth of democracy and the rise of scientific industry. This aspiration has been and is being resisted, sometimes openly, sometimes subtly, but as an aim it has been formally acknowledged, almost universally' (Williams 1965, 11).

Addendum

This chapter was originally written in April 2015. One month later, the Conservative party won a slim majority at the UK General Election. The new government published a green paper in November. "Fulfilling Our Potential: Teaching Excellence, Social Mobility and Student Choice" (BIS 2015) outlined a new Teaching Excellence Framework (TEF), which in its first phase would assess universities and colleges offering HE against a set of metrics. Separately, from 2017, data based on earnings and benefits made available by the Small Business, Enterprise and Employment Act is to be published.

Institutions achieving the baseline performance in the TEF would be allowed to increase their tuition fees in line with inflation (capped by a new maximum tuition fee above the £9,000 limit frozen since 2012). In subsequent years, the government intends to introduce up to three TEF 'levels', with the expectation that fees will 'increasingly differentiate'; different TEF levels would entitle institutions to raise their fees by different fractions of inflation each year. A Higher Education Bill setting out these measures was put before parliament in the summer of 2016.

As I predicted in the original chapter, the government also froze the loan repayment threshold at £21,000 and thus established the principle of actively managing the loan 'book' (the threshold will be reviewed every five years). This measure was combined with changes to the calculations used to value loans in the government accounts—reducing the average official 'loss' on loans issued annually from 45 percent to 20-25 percent. Further savings will be achieved by abolishing maintenance grants for all new starters in September 2016. Those who would have been eligible for grants will now be entitled to more loans.

Notes

1. This is a companion paper to McGettigan 2015. What is outlined here as performance is coeval with the kind of data the private sector wants in order to price loan-assets.

2. 'Estimating Human Capital of Graduates' Project website: https://www.ifs .org.uk/research_areas/38/41/195?year_published[start]=&year_published [end]=&page=1&.

3. What is often missed—for example, by Foucault (2004)—is that the family in Gary Becker's work is reconceived as a Coasian intergenerational firm making investment decisions. Social mobility is then accordingly calibrated so that no individual should be hamstrung by the decisions of their parents and antecedents. *Socioeconomic status* (SES) is therefore a counter-concept to *class*. In a society with high social mobility, SES can always be revised by good investment decisions—there is no systematic disadvantage—and the situation is competitive. Long-run inequality is not determined by class if access to capital is not constrained. Therefore, the role for government is to ensure that the human capital markets are functional and thus inherited advantage is minimised. (Even better if the market allows children to borrow as individuals rather than families on their behalf). This gives some content to Thatcher's 'there are individuals and there are families' statement and reveals the self-conception of David Willetts's *The Pinch* (2010), in which demographic cohorts, 'generations', is a third factor introduced to the analysis. We need to attend to *familia œconomica* rather than *homo œconomicus*.

4. 'Over the 10 years 1993 to 2003, average graduate earnings grew by an average 0.9% per year in real terms. Given the decline in real earnings associated with the recent financial crisis and recession, average graduate earnings actually declined over the period 1993 to 2012—equivalent to an

average 0.2% decline per year over the 19 years. The real growth in average graduate earnings in recent decades has therefore been lower than the 1.1% a year real average earnings growth assumed by the [Office for Budgetary Responsibility] for the long run. However, this lack of growth in average earnings *might be due to changes in the composition of graduates: as more individuals obtain degrees, the average quality of degrees may have declined'* (Crawford, Crawford, and Jin 2014; my emphasis).

5. Note that from a free market perspective, cross-subsidies, whether of subject to subject or teaching to research and vice versa, are a problem for this reason. The government is not anti-arts and humanities, but is very much exercised by fees set at £9,000 rather than close to the presumed 'cost base'. The preference for free markets also explains why the Treasury decided to remove undergraduate recruitment controls entirely from universities for 2015 entry: Restricting places leads to unmet demand, which keeps prices high.

References

Becker, G. 1991. *A Treatise on the Family*. Enlarged edition. Cambridge, MA: Harvard University Press.

Britton, J., L. Dearden, N. Shephard, and A. Vignoles. 2016. "How English-Domiciled Graduate Earnings Vary with Gender, Institution Attended, Subject and Socio-economic Background." Working Paper W16/06, Institute for Fiscal Studies, London. http://www.nuffieldfoundation.org/sites/default/files/files/wp1606.pdf.

Conservatives. 2015. "The Conservative Party Manifesto 2015." https://s3-eu -west-1.amazonaws.com/manifesto2015/ConservativeManifesto2015.pdf.

Crawford, C., R. Crawford, and W. Jin. 2014. "Estimating the Public Cost of Student Loans." *Institute for Fiscal Studies* (April).

Department for Business, Innovation & Skills (BIS). 2015. "Fulfilling Our Potential: Teaching Excellence, Social Mobility and Student Choice." November. https://www.gov.uk/government/uploads/system/uploads/attachment_data/file/474227/BIS-15-623-fulfilling-our-potential-teaching -excellence-social-mobility-and-student-choice.pdf.

Department for Business, Innovation & Skills and the Prime Minister's Office (BIS/PMO). 2014. "Enterprise for All: The Relevance of Enterprise in

Education." June 19. https://www.gov.uk/government/publications/enterprise-for-all-the-relevance-of-enterprise-in-education.

Foucault, M. 2004. *The Birth of Biopolitics: Lectures at the Collège de France 1978–79*. Edited by Michel Senellart and translated by Graham Burchell. Basingstoke: Palgrave Macmillan.

Friedman, M. 1955. "Role for Government in Education." https://www.edchoice.org/who-we-are/our-founders/the-friedmans-on-school-choice/article/the-role-of-government-in-education/.

McGettigan, A. 2013. *The Great University Gamble: Money, Markets and the Future of Higher Education*. London: Pluto.

McGettigan, A. 2015. "The Treasury View of Higher Education: Student Loans, Illiquid Assets and Fiscal Control." In *Forging Economic Discovery in 21st Century Britain*, edited by J. Montgomerie, 47–51. London: Political Economy Research Centre.

UK Government. 2015a. "Small Business, Enterprise and Employment Act 2015, Part 6." http://www.legislation.gov.uk/ukpga/2015/26/part/6/enacted.

UK Government. 2015b. "Small Business, Enterprise and Employment Act: Education Evaluation Fact Sheet." https://www.gov.uk/government/uploads/system/uploads/attachment_data/file/363503/bis-14-1135-sbee-bill-education-evaluation-fact-sheet.pdf.

Willetts, D. 2010. *The Pinch: How the Baby Boomers Stole their Children's Future—and Why They Should Give It Back*. London: Atlantic Books.

Willetts, D. 2011. "We Cannot Be Certain about Every Step. But the Journey Will Be Worthwhile." *Times Higher Education*, May 26. www.timeshighereducation.co.uk/story.asp?storycode=416257.

Willetts, D. 2012. "Wake Up to the New World, Declares Willetts." *Times Higher Education*, October 11. http://www.timeshighereducation.co.uk/421448.article.

Willetts, D. 2013. *Robbins Revisited: Bigger and Better Higher Education*. London: Social Market Foundation.

Williams, R. 1965. *The Long Revolution*. London: Pelican Books.

9

The Coalition Government's Cuts to Legal Aid: Who Is Counting the Cost?

Roger Smith

The Italian poet Dante, in the middle of his life, famously found himself lost in a dark and overgrown wood in which he lost the direct path. In the end, things turned out well enough and he created one of the great works of world literature. His experience is not that dissimilar to anyone seeking to work through the economic, social and political consequences of cuts to the Legal Aid, Sentencing and Punishment of Offenders (LASPO) Act of 2012. Such investigators are, however, unlikely to turn misfortune to such good effect. There is not—indeed, without more work, could not be—any really authoritative examination of the consequences. We have some indication from authoritative sources such as the National Audit Office (NAO), but those who argue how extreme the cuts are need to develop better ways of demonstrating that if there is to be a hope of getting any successor government to reel them back to any degree beyond the marginal.

This is not to say that the legal aid forest isle is not full of noise. Echoing through it are the screams of bruised providers whose funding has been cut and ire raised; they proffer a clear assertion—though often little proof—of the consequences in terms of human misery, the cost to the economy and other government departments (LASPO 2014). But hanging in the air is also the deep boom of official statements, all basically variations of 'we don't know and we don't care'. As it was put to the House of Commons Public Accounts Committee: 'The Ministry told us that it was not possible to know what the impact of the reforms might be outside of the Ministry. We heard from the Treasury Officer of Accounts that impact assessments often do not quantify costs of politic changes to the wider public sector . . . the Ministry told us that the failure to monetise potential knock-on costs of reforms is "representative of a common pattern seen across government"' (HoC 2015, para. 22).

There is no shortage of voices trilling the need for more research—from the majestic thunder of the NAO to the high-pitched squeak of academics. From the former: 'The Ministry of Justice is on track to make significant and quick reductions in its spending on civil legal aid. However, it has been slower to think through how and why people access civil legal aid; the scale of the additional costs to the Ministry likely to be generated by people choosing to represent themselves; and the impact on the ability and willingness of providers to provide legal services for the fees paid. Without this understanding, the Ministry's implementation of the reforms to civil legal aid cannot be said to have delivered better overall value for money for the taxpayer' (NAO 2014). And as an example of the latter: 'There was universal agreement in the literature that advice results in positive outcomes for clients and their households. However, almost all of the evidence originated from the 'grey literature', i.e., informally published work, where the quality of the evidence was generally poor. For instance, only a handful of reports were able to provide detailed information on the data, a clear and robust methodology, and sound analysis from which they draw their conclusions. A clear problem throughout the literature was the lack of a consistent or universally adopted measure of outcome or quality' (Cookson and Mold 2014).

A debate on the consequences of the LASPO cuts segues into a wider discussion of the economic costs and benefits of legal aid more generally. The legal services program in the United States was launched as part of an explicit anti-poverty objective, and there has been consistent interest in how you might measure effectiveness ever since—both in the United States and elsewhere (Houseman and Minhoff 2014). The jury remains out, however, and the need for further research is acknowledged even by those in the thick of advancing the economic benefits of legal aid.

Therefore, the consequences of the LASPO cuts raise difficult issues of a political, theoretical and practical nature encountered both in this jurisdiction and abroad. Let us try to limit these by way of the following opening definitions and limitations:

1. This chapter is concerned primarily with the effect of the LASPO cuts—that is, the following ways in which the government intended to make savings from the legal aid budget—all of which came on stream around or about early 2013: the removal of most civil legal aid and advice, save for (tightly defined) cases of domestic violence and some other matters (largely those protected by the European Convention on Human Rights and the Human Rights Act);[1] the introduction of a 'mandatory' telephone 'gateway' for some residual areas of advice; raising the merits test; reduction in financial eligibility; tightening of the conditions for judicial review applications; and reductions in

remuneration (HoC 2013). Other issues, such as wider restrictions to judicial review (in which arena battles continue), costs reform (the aftermath of the 'Jackson' report) or even local authority funding cuts are not considered—even though they are obviously linked. However, the catastrophic fall in the number of tribunal applications is referred to ahead since it may, at least in part, be related to the reduction of legal aid availability and was abruptly manifest in the first quarter of 2013.

2. Within the LASPO cuts, this chapter is concerned with the consequences for those who would formerly have received legal aid and advice. The cuts removed around £300 million from the public funding of providers. This has had a massive effect in terms of those providers who concentrated on civil legal aid both in private practice and in law centres or other NGOs. Many in the latter category were simply wiped out or, at the very least, had to cut back completely on their legal aid work. Charting the wider effect of that slashing of provision is left for another forum.

3. Preference deliberately has been given to 'official' or (allegedly) 'neutral' sources of information—such as the reports of the House of Commons Public Accounts Committee or the NAO—over the assertions of providers or former providers, for obvious reasons. However, objective hard statistics are hard to find from any sources. Nevertheless, it should be noted that a stream of studies emanating largely from the advice sector in this country, and the legal sector more internationally, assert methodologies sufficient to allow reasonable calculation. Citizens Advice, for example, calculated the return per pound spent on legal aid for housing advice as £2.34 (Citizens Advice 2010). As to the consequences of the LASPO cuts, let us take the figures from the report of the NAO for a definitive statement:

- £300 million: NAO estimate of spending reduction in 2013–2014 from the LASPO reforms

- £268 million: NAO estimate of expected annual reduction in spending as a result of LASPO reforms

- 685,459: Civil legal aid matters the Legal Aid Agency would have been expected to approve in 2013–2014 without the reforms

- 361,551: Civil legal aid matters the agency expected to approve in 2013–2014 as a result of the reforms

- 300,496: Civil legal aid matters actually approved in 2013–2014 (17 percent fewer than expected)

- 18,519, or 30 percent: Increase in the number of cases starting in the family courts in which neither party had representation

- 9,000: Increase in family mediation assessments that the Ministry of Justice expected in 2013–2014

- 17,246, or 56 percent: Decrease in family mediation assessments in the year after the reforms (NOA 2014)

The picture, overall, is of cuts even more severe than were initially expected. The savings were over £30 million (around 10 percent) more than expected. The fall in the number of cases was greater by 17 percent than expected. Family mediations fell by more than half when they were expected to grow. Thus, the cuts themselves had a wider 'chilling' effect on provision, which meant that even those theoretically still within scope failed to claim entitled aid. The effect of the cuts (linked with related issues such as rises in tribunal fees and small claims court costs) can be seen in related statistics.

First, all tribunal appeals (except those relating to immigration) fell off a cliff in the second quarter of 2013. The Ministry of Justice reported that HMCTS Tribunals recorded 74,401 receipts in the period from April to June 2014. This is down 16 percent from the previous quarter and 71 percent compared with the same period from 2013 (Ministry of Justice 2014, 8).

To some extent, this fall is due to procedural diversion from appeals through mandatory review in the case of social security or referral to ACAS in employment. However, the ministry was forced to acknowledge a likely explanation for the latter: Fees for employment tribunals and the employment appeals tribunal were introduced for claims received on or after July 29, 2013, alongside wider reform of procedural rules (following the Underhill Review of Employment Tribunal Rules; Ministry of Justice 2014). As for the consequences of mandatory social security review, the ministry reported that robust data was not yet available to assess the impact of these changes on tribunal receipts (Ministry of Justice 2014).

Second, there is evidence of displacement. An advice structure, underfunded and under pressure, still exists to take some degree of overflow from the cuts to legal aid. The NAO noted:

> Some individuals who are no longer eligible for civil legal aid may choose to pay for legal advice themselves. However, many who would have received legal aid are unlikely to be able to afford full legal advice or representation for their case. The Ministry acknowledged it was likely that more individuals would seek free advice from third-sector providers because of the

reforms. It did not try to forecast the extra demand for these services.

Our consultation with providers indicates that third-sector providers may not be able to meet the extra demand generated by the reforms. Among legal firms/advocate respondents, 49% told us they were referring more clients to third-sector organisations since April 2013 and 70% of third-sector respondents told us they could meet half or less of the demand from clients who were not eligible for civil legal aid.

This finding is consistent with other recent research. For example, Citizens Advice reports that there has been a 62% increase in people seeking advice online about help with legal costs since the reforms, while 92% of Citizens Advice Bureaux are finding it difficult to refer people to specialist legal advice since the reforms were implemented. Similarly, the Bar Pro Bono Unit reports that requests for assistance have increased by almost 50% since April 2013. (NAO 2014, 25)

Third, we have evidence that increasing numbers of people are representing themselves—presumably from the beginning of a case, for which we would have no data—through to litigation. This was recognised by both the Public Accounts Committee and the NAO—from the former:

In the year following the reforms, there was an increase of 18,519 cases (30%) in which both parties were representing themselves (known as litigants in person or LIPs) in family courts. Within this, there were 8,110 more cases involving contact with children in which both parties were LIPs in 2013–14, an increase of 89% from the previous year. Judges have estimated that cases involving LIPs can take 50% longer and many legal professionals have said that they place additional demands upon court staff. The NAO also identified an increase in the number of contested family cases reaching the courts, with the figure rising from 64% in 2012–13 to 89% in 2013–14. We heard evidence from the Magistrates' Association that magistrates feel that the significant rise in the number of LIPs in family courts has had a negative impact on the administration of justice. (HoC 2015, 13)

The NAO was willing to put a figure on the cost of this growth in self-representation, though its methodology is probably somewhat rough and ready: 'Based on the increase in self-representation, we estimate the additional cost to HM Courts & Tribunals Service at £3 million per year, plus direct costs to the Ministry of approximately £400,000 . . . There may also be costs to the wider public sector if people whose problems could have been resolved by legal aid-funded advice suffer adverse consequences to their health and wellbeing as a result of no longer having access to legal aid' (HoC 2015, 6).

Fourth, some people may just lose out. The Public Accounts Committee reported: 'We heard from the Magistrates' Association that some people have difficulties with the court forms and processes involved in family law matters. For example, the application form for a case involving contact with children is 24 pages long, and the guidance document for that form is 32 pages long. The Magistrates' Association told us that this complexity may prevent people from accessing support to maintain a relationship with their children' (HoC 2015, 12).

The cuts have clearly had an influence beyond themselves. Solicitors evidently played a major role in encouraging mediation in family cases. Even though funding remains, the number of cases going to mediation has slumped: 'The Ministry continues to fund mediation through civil legal aid and expected 9,000 more mediation assessments and 10,000 more mediations to start in 2013–14. However, mediation assessments fell by more than 17,000 and there were more than 5,000 fewer mediations starting in 2013–14 than there were in 2012–13' (NAO 2014, para. 10).

Both the NAO and the Public Accounts Committee criticised the Ministry of Justice's lack of perspective beyond simply delivering the cuts to its legal aid budget. The NAO recommended the following:

a. The Ministry should develop measures to evaluate the impact of the reforms more fully, including estimating any wider costs to the courts system. For example, it should improve its data on court case duration, potentially as part of its criminal justice system efficiency programme.

b. The Ministry should consider what further steps it could take to meet its objective of reducing the number of cases going to courts in the areas of law removed from the scope of civil legal aid. This includes continuing to monitor the use of mediation, and considering what further action it should take if take-up does not increase in line with expectations.

c. The Ministry should establish the extent to which those who are eligible for civil legal aid are able to access it and what obstacles, if any, exist.

d. The Ministry should develop its understanding of the challenges facing civil legal aid providers and the provision of support across the country. It should use this improved understanding to ensure sustainability in the market and coverage across the country. (NAO 2014, para. 17)

In calling for more research on impact measures, the NAO joins just about every interested institution or researcher in the field. As Cookson and Mold commented on evidence to the Low Commission: 'Primarily, there is a need for further evaluation of advice services, to determine their effectiveness and value for money. Currently there is an absence of good-quality research on the economic value of legal aid, focusing on costs of services and return of investment, especially research based in the UK. More quantitative, longitudinal studies are warranted in this area' (NAO 2014, para. 17).

The study referred to earlier is demanding about the methodology of what needs to be done:

'Many of the economic benefit and Social Return on Investment studies make inadequately supported assumptions in the course of describing the cost savings resulting from legal services. A classic example of an inadequately supported assertion is the assertion that a certain percentage of people who legal services attorneys saved from eviction or from having their mortgage foreclosed would have had to go into emergency housing had it not been for the legal services intervention. Because little research has been done on the number of people who resort to emergency housing in the absence of a legal services intervention, the economic benefits studies rely on a single, small, outdated study from New York State to suggest that somewhere in the neighborhood of 20 percent of homeless people resort to emergency housing. An updated study, tracking people evicted from rental housing or mortgage foreclosure, would offer us a much more realistic picture of what actually would have happened to people evicted or whose mortgages were foreclosed. A corollary study could examine what happened to people who were not evicted." (Houseman and Minhoff 2014, 50)

Any comprehensive study of the impact of the LASPO cuts would require at least three elements: First, an analysis of the economic consequences undertaken with the rigour suggested previously. We don't really have the data to go beyond assertion at the present time, and the truth is that we may never be able to get absolutely reliable figures—but we should certainly try. Approaches do not have to be drily mathematical. It may be possible to find areas in the country where the effects have been mitigated—through the provision of pro bono services or with funding from local authorities or foundations—which can be compared with areas where the cuts bit as intended. If these cuts are ever to be ameliorated, we need more than assertion to back up our argument—even if we are addressing ourselves to a more sympathetic government than the present.

Second, we need to chart, if we can, the consequences of the cuts in terms of social exclusion and community (in)cohesion. What is the experience of women excluded from legal aid during divorce? What are the consequences for their children? Third, we need to identify the decline in public accountability that arises from the reduction of appeal, review and challenge rights. At stake here are some of the great gains of the 'welfare rights' movement, which shifted the discourse from discretionary donation to legally backed entitlement. Can we achieve this third aim? Undoubtedly not perfectly, but the attempt will help us do our best in the struggle to preserve services and to regain them.

Finally, the ultimate test of a legal aid scheme for the poor is how well 'justiciable problems' might be resolved at all levels of society. We need something like the British Crime Survey, which nationally charts whether people are finding it easier or harder to resolve their legal problems. Here, we do have a methodology—developed by Hazel Genn (Genn 1990)—which was used by the Legal Services Research Centre before it was abolished as part of the LASPO cuts. This methodology was followed around the world.

Somebody needs to fund surveys that allow comparison of access to justice over time—but don't hold your breath. It won't be this government that does it. Who, then, will take up the role of the Dante of the justice system? The role is vacant; the need is pressing.

Note

1. The remaining issues in scope contained specified matters in relation to actions against the police, clinical negligence (only neurological damage to

infants), community care, debt, discrimination, education, family (very limited), housing (also very limited), immigration and asylum (again very limited), mental health, various miscellaneous matters, public law, and welfare benefits (very limited).

References

Citizens Advice. 2010. "Towards a Business Case for Legal Aid." Paper presented at the Legal Services Research Centre's eighth international research conference, London, July. https://namati.org/resources/citizens -advice-towards-a-business-case-for-legal-aid/.

Cookson, G., and F. Mold. 2014. "Low Commission: The Business Case for Social Welfare Advice Services: An Evidence Review." Lay summary, University of Surrey, July/August.

Genn, H. 1990. *Paths to Justice: What People Do and Think about Going to Law*. London: Hart Publishing.

HoC (House of Commons). 2013. "House of Commons Library Civil Legal Aid: Changes since 1 April 2013."

HoC (House of Commons). 2015. "Implementing Reforms of Civil Legal Aid." House of Commons Committee of Public Accounts, HC 808, February 4.

Houseman, A., and E. Minhoff. 2014. "The Anti-Poverty Effects of Civil Legal Aid." Public Welfare Foundation, October 2014. http://legalaidresearch.org/ wp-content/uploads/Houseman-Anti-Poverty-Effects-Civil-Legal-Aid.pdf.

LASPO. 2014. "Review of Evidence to the LASPO Act Enquiry": *Legal Action*, June.

Ministry of Justice. 2014. "Tribunals Statistics Quarterly: April to June 2014." Ministry of Justice, September 11. https://www.gov.uk/government/uploads/ system/uploads/attachment_data/file/352914/tribunal-statistics-quarterly -april-june-2014.pdf.

National Audit Office (NAO). 2014. "Implementing Reforms to Civil Legal Aid." http://www.nao.org.uk/wp-content/uploads/2014/11/Implementing-reforms -to-civil-legal-aid1.pdf.

10

Public Libraries in the Age of Austerity: The Gloves Are Off

Ian Anstice

Since 2010, British public libraries have been undergoing the most difficult period in their peacetime history. Before the coalition government came into power, public libraries had been experiencing static or increasing budgets combined with stable or reduced levels of usage (DCMS 2012). Large-scale projects to refurbish central libraries had restarted in Liverpool and Manchester, and the largest ever English public library rebuild had started in Birmingham. Now, the sector is facing deep and sustained budget cuts, with hundreds of small libraries under threat of closure or passing to volunteers and even the new Library of Birmingham confronted with a deep crisis (BBC 2015). Facing this disaster, the old certainties have been washed away, with the role of paid staff, council involvement and even the library itself being called into question.

Contrary to what can be gleaned from much of the media, the last five years has not seen a dramatic number of library closures. According to Cipfa figures (Cipfa 2015), there were 423 fewer libraries in 2015/2016 than there were in 2010/2011, out of an original total of 4,340. This figure, representing nearly 10 percent of buildings, is quite impressively high over a five-year period, but nowhere near the massacre present in public perception. Moreover, these closures are not just simple reactions to budget cuts. Rather, as in the case of the London Borough of Brent, they were part of a deliberate strategy to concentrate funding on a smaller number of branches, improving those branches and thus maintaining usage (Anstice 2012).

That's not to say the cuts aren't real; in fact, they're far deeper than 10 percent. Indeed, there has been an overall reduction in budget of at least 20 percent over the same time period, which, depending on how one factors in inflation, could mean a cut of up to 40 percent in real terms. Bear in mind as well that certain authorities have cut their budgets far deeper than this average. What then accounts for the relatively small number of closures? Public library authorities, of which there are 151 in England alone, have found many ways to reduce expenditures without closing libraries. A term commonly used by campaigners for this approach is the evocative *hollowing out* (Ellis 2013). This can include all manner of reductions, notably in opening hours, in staffing and in book funds (Davies 2013). Somerset, which retreated from closing eleven branches and four mobiles due to a lost court case, instead lost staff, introduced self-service machines and volunteer staff, and moved services into co-located buildings (Public Libraries News 2015c). Other authorities have used a mixture of these approaches in conjunction with reducing the book fund. Obviously, such responses frequently lead to reductions. By not closing some of its buildings in a time of budget reduction, a council can simply discourage library usage, which then weakens the case for keeping them open overall.

As well as cutting expenditure, attempts have been made to increase income (Naylor 2014), with one of the most frequently mentioned options that of installing a cafe. Although this can be successful for income in popular and busy locations, the costs of running such a retail arm means that profit cannot be guaranteed. There are also concerns about the over-commercialization of libraries (SPPL 2012), which have long been valued as neutral, welcoming spaces in which, almost uniquely on the High Street, one does not need to spend money.

In addition, councils have been outsourcing public library service to other organisations, although inroads by the private sector have been very limited. The sole example is Carillion, which runs four library services, albeit via a non-profit arm. Far more libraries have been passed to non-profit trusts, with the most prominent being GLL (Public Libraries News 2015a). Two other library services (York and Suffolk) are run as mutuals.

Along with library closures, the other response to budget cuts attracting high media attention is the passing of branches to volunteers. From a handful prior to 2010, there are now at least 384 such libraries in the UK (Public Libraries News 2015b), with more planned. Although replacing paid staff with volunteers is rarely claimed to be an actual improvement, local library users may reluctantly feel forced to become volunteers in order to keep their libraries open. Indeed, some users have complained of being blackmailed (News Hound 2011) by local authorities into the move. Councils can argue that if a local community does not wish to volunteer to run its local library, then they don't really want it (Dorset Echo 2012). More tellingly, the issue of volunteering can split campaign groups into two or even co-opt those protesting against cuts onto the council side in an attempt to rescue the service. The success of some volunteer libraries, at least in the short term, encourages councils to withdraw from more, even though there are concerns about the future of such initiatives in the longer term (NFWI Research 2013). There is also concern that volunteer libraries (confusingly called *community libraries* by many councils) further atomise a larger library service, because each becomes run as a separate organisation.

Public protest against public library closures has been strong, but often ineffective. Consultations on public library closures are commonly reported to be the most responded to of all council consultations, but also often have little effect. Within days of cuts being formally announced, campaign groups spontaneously form in the affected areas, either from library users or from pre-existing Friends of the Library groups. Such groups have a variety of weapons at their disposal, from placarding council offices to protest marches to petitions. If all else fails, campaigners can and do take councils to court via judicial reviews. This time-consuming and expensive business has led to several notable turnarounds by councils such as those in Somerset or Moray. But, in other cases, decisions have gone against campaigners even if they have made initial wins, such as recently in Lincolnshire. In all instances, the councils are likely to blame the campaigners for the cost of legal action, even if they are found to have been acting improperly.

National responses to cuts in public libraries have varied depending on the groups involved. Those organisations that see themselves as tied to government or local government have met the challenge with pragmatism. The Society of Chief Librarians (SCL), the membership of which is formed of senior library officers, tailors its publicity to promote libraries as fitting in with government agendas. It even welcomes the replacement of paid staff with volunteers as long as they are 'professionally managed'. The Arts Council England (ACE)—which, as well as encouraging best practice, is funded by the government to distribute grants for projects to libraries—can also be relied upon to rarely, if ever, directly challenge the government's position. The Chartered Institute of Library and Information Professionals (CILIP), on the other hand, while also wanting to associate libraries with government aims in order to stress their importance, is more likely to protest, especially in recent years. The group is a member of the Speak Up for Libraries coalition and has adopted a stance formally against the replacement of paid staff. The Unison and Unite trade unions are far more likely to protest against cuts, which directly affect their members, as is the national campaign group the Library Campaign.

Stung with criticism over cuts to library services, the DCMS response has been either to deny the impact of cuts (Flood 2012) or to conduct research into best practice within the sector. What it has not done, which has caused much anger amongst campaigners, is to intervene in any library authority, regardless of the severity of the cuts proposed. The 1964 Public Libraries and Museums Act gives the secretary of state the power to order a review and ultimately take over the running of a library service if it is not meeting its obligation to provide a 'comprehensive and efficient service'. However, the minister responsible for libraries throughout this period, MP Ed Vaizey, has steadfastly refused to rule against the actions of any authority. As such, councils consider library services a 'soft' statutory service, with councillors even sometimes failing to know that they are statutory at all. Indeed, it is notable that almost all legal challenges by local groups against cuts have concentrated instead on other legislation, usually in the areas of equality and human rights.

What is apparent to any serious observer of public libraries over the last six years is that, when push comes to the shove, the need to reduce funding normally takes precedence over local protest and legal protections. It does not matter how many thousands respond to a consultation or protest in marches; if the council has decided on a course of action, then that is what will happen. The protection of the courts, in a service such as that of libraries in which legal precedent is limited and definitions are weak, is haphazard at best. Central government has shown itself impervious to appeal when it comes to cuts to library services. It is also dedicated to allowing local councils to find their own solution, and is unwilling to impose strategies or reorganisation on the multitude of local library authorities and the hundreds of new volunteer libraries. In other words, the old certainties of public libraries being a public good, protected by popularity and government, have gone. It is up to each authority to determine how best to respond to budget reductions, and, if said authority decides that cutting libraries is a valid response, then there is little than can effectively be done to stop it.

References

Anstice, I. 2012. "Concentrate on Services, Not Usage." Public Libraries News, September 9. http://www.publiclibrariesnews.com/2012/09/concentrate-on-services-not-buildings-councillor-powney-on-brents-library-transformation-project.html.

BBC. 2015. "Birmingham Library Opening Hours Nearly Halved." BBC, February 10. http://www.bbc.co.uk/news/uk-england-birmingham-31354592.

Cipfa. 2015. "Public Libraries." http://www.cipfa.org/services/statistics/comparative-profiles/public-libraries.

Davies, S. 2013. "The Damage: The Public Library Service under Attack." Unison, June. https://www.unison.org.uk/content/uploads/2013/06/On-line -Catalogue215893.pdf.

DCMS (Department for Culture, Media & Sport). 2012. "Taking Part 2011/12: Annual Adult and Child Release." https://www.gov.uk/government/statistics/ taking-part-the-national-survey-of-culture-leisure-and-sport-adult-and -child-report-2011-12.

Dorset Echo. 2012. "Mobile Library Will Replace Portland's Underhill Facility." *Dorset Echo*, April 24. http://www.dorsetecho.co.uk/news/9666042 .Mobile_library_will_replace_Portland_s_Underhill_facility/.

Ellis, M. 2013. "Two Libraries a Week Closed Due to Tory Cuts." *Mirror*, March 4. http://www.mirror.co.uk/news/uk-news/two-libraries-week-being- closed-1741438.

Flood, A. 2012. "Ed Vaizey Says Libraries 'Thriving' and Rejects Prediction of 600 Closures." *Guardian*, June 29. http://www.theguardian.com/books/2012/ jun/29/ed-vaizey-libraries-600-closures.

Naylor, A. 2014. "Income Generation for Public Libraries: A Practical Guide for Library Service Commissioners in England." Locality, July 22. http://locality.org .uk/blog/income-generation-public-libraries-practical-guide-library-service/.

News Hound. 2011. "This Is Not Volunteering, It Is Blackmail!" Ivo, September 29. http://ivo.org/post/this-is-not-volunteering-it-is-blackmail- 548768a1910868620765983d.

NFWI Research. 2013. "On Permanent Loan? Community Managed Libraries: The Volunteer Perspective." NFWI Research, January. http://www.thewi.org .uk/__data/assets/pdf_file/0006/49848/on-permanent-loan.pdf.

Public Libraries News. 2015a. "List of Library Trusts and Prospective Library Trusts." Public Libraries News. http://www.publiclibrariesnews.com/about -public-libraries-news/trusts-current-uk-situation.

Public Libraries News. 2015b. "List of UK Volunteer Libraries." Public Libraries News. http://www.publiclibrariesnews.com/about-public-libraries-news/ list-of-uk-volunteer-run-libraries.

Public Libraries News. 2015c. "Sheffield to Southampton." Public Libraries News. http://www.publiclibrariesnews.com/about-public-libraries-news/ information/oxfordshire-to-yorkshire/sheffield-to-southampton.

Wylie, A. 2012. "Extreme Income Generation: The New Reality?" Stop the Privatisation of Public Libraries, December 5. http://dontprivatiselibraries .blogspot.co.uk/2012/12/extreme-income-generation-new-reality.html.

The Corruption of News and Information in Markets

The finger of blame for the financial crisis of 2007–2008 has been pointed in several directions—from greedy bankers to incompetent regulators and self-serving governments—but clearly the breakdown in financial news, information and communication also played a key part. All markets need reliable information in order to attract and service buyers and sellers. In theory, this information should be equally distributed to all parties. However, market participants always look for a market edge, which often involves getting inside information early, spreading faulty information to others or obscuring the true financial picture through clever accounting and complex financial instruments. Thus, the scandals, bubbles and crashes that began to multiply after several rounds of financial deregulation in the 1980s and 1990s have continued unabated since 2008, despite various attempts at reform. At the same time, successful public prosecutions of individuals remain extremely rare, and financial sector pay and bonuses continue to rise to extravagant levels.

Chapter 11 focuses on the corruption of information flows in the London Stock Exchange, in which, supposedly, all market participants have been given equal access to the same information. However, as Philip Augar argues, ever since the London stock market was deregulated in the 1980s, this has not been the case. Investment banks have been able to take advantage of their central positions in the trading and information chains to keep making large profits at the expense of all others. Even after the financial crisis and new waves of financial regulation, that crucial problem remains.

In chapter 12, Peter Thompson shows that many years after the financial crisis hit, problems remain as deep-seated as ever. He uncovers the details of how the Libor scandal came about and the failures of financial news reporters and regulators to deal with the problem earlier. Although focusing on Libor, the chapter also sheds light on the reasons why so few failed to spot (or report on) the coming financial crisis of 2007–2008, as well as why future crises are also likely to be missed. The continuing problem is that both journalists and regulators are dependent on self-serving inside sources for key information, as well as for interpretation of that information.

In chapter 13, Henry Silke demonstrates how the mainstream Irish press contributed to the property bubble that helped crash the Irish economy in 2007–2008. The rapid rise of the Irish economy was strongly tied to promoting the real estate boom and encouraging international investors and businesses to come to Ireland. In the process, a property bubble grew, which then made homes unaffordable for most people while also destabilising the economy. The media, with close links to both elite national political and international investment networks, first pumped up the bubble and then kept it inflated. Thus, mainstream media coverage of the housing market, supposedly constructed for the public, was instead produced by and for market-linked interests.

11

The Edge: Investment Banks and Information Flows in Public Markets

Philip Augar

If there was any benefit from the recent banking crisis and great recession, it was to increase public knowledge of financial markets. The world learned the hard way about bankers' greed and incompetence and began to understand the power conferred by the market information they possess. The collapse of the US investment bank Lehman Brothers in 2008 and the disastrous knock-on effects for the world economy due to the demise of this apparently peripheral institution brought home the central role played by investment banks in our financial ecosystem. Their influence is immense, and any discussion of information flows within public markets needs to start in their dealing rooms.

The deregulation of Wall Street in 1975 and the City of London in 1986 introduced an integrated model of investment banking that channelled powerful information flows into these financial institutions. Single firms were able to provide advisory services both for investors who buy shares and for the corporations who issue them, giving firms the privileged position of working on both sides of a trade. These same institutions were also allowed to trade for clients and for their own profit. It thus became possible for them to work for the buyer and the seller in a single deal and simultaneously to make a proprietary trading profit.

Regulators have tinkered with this model over the years, but the investment banks' information advantage remains intact, giving them a birds'-eye view of markets. This privileged position is at the heart of an asymmetrical financial system in which the dice are loaded against the end users. Every line of market business that is tradable flows through the investment banks' dealing rooms, and with that information comes extraordinary market power. Sometimes, the temptation to abuse that privileged position proves irresistible and insider trading and market manipulation occur, but cheating is scarcely necessary; there are rich pickings for legitimate operators who obey the rules.

There is a paragraph in *Den of Thieves* (Stewart 1991, 352), journalist James B. Stewart's classic account of Wall Street's scandals of the 1980s, that reveals this advantage. Stewart describes a conversation between Robert Freeman, at the time head of arbitrage at Goldman Sachs, and another trader. Freeman reflects 'that when he was younger, he loved to go to Las Vegas to gamble. But now, he says, he doesn't like casino odds. "It's not fun anymore. I guess I've been in this business too long" he says, "I'm used to having an edge"'.

Freeman had put his finger on it. The financial behemoths' edge is knowledge and integration. At any given moment in time, giant investment banks know more about the state of the world economy than any other public or private organization. The remarkable thing is not that sometimes they abuse this power but that they fail to take more advantage of it.

The last quarter of the twentieth century was the golden age of investment banking and revealed what the model could produce. In that period, profits in the US securities industry grew by a towering twenty-six times, quadruple the rate of increase in America's corporate profits and GDP over the same period. Extending the analysis to 2004 and smoothing profits to adjust for annual volatility, securities industry profits grew at a compound growth rate of 10 percent per annum, compared with a compound growth rate of 7 percent per annum in both US nominal GDP and corporate profits and 4 percent per annum for consumer price inflation (Augar 2006, 52).

Although practitioners believe that this performance was achieved as a result of their own genius, the reality is that it was produced by legitimately exploiting generous rules that provided superior knowledge and the ability to borrow heavily to leverage their bets. All they had to do to preserve this model was not get too greedy—but that was a temptation that Wall Street's alpha males could not resist.

The work of New York State Attorney General Eliot Spitzer from 2001 to 2002 exposed the scams that the investment banks had been running during the dotcom initial public offering (IPO) bubble. Following Spitzer's revelations, tougher rules were introduced to create internal barriers between the different departments of investment banks. Undeterred by the rising tide of regulation in one area of their business, the banks looked for new places that they could use their edge, adopting such tactics as selling over-valued mortgage-backed securities to less knowledgeable clients and secretly betting against them in a 'heads we win, tails you lose' trade. The banking crisis of 2007–2008 exposed this malpractice and prompted regulators to dig deeper into banks' activities, revealing various other dark corners, including the manipulation of market benchmarks such as Libor and other inter-bank borrowing rates.

The investment banks had spoiled their own party. By over-leveraging, they were financially ruined in the crash, and by cheating, they created such a tide of adverse public opinion that traditionally friendly regulators and legislators had no option but to tighten the rules. Where does that leave information flows and probity within public markets now?

As a result of more intense supervision, new regulations and the deterrent effect of punishments, markets are currently in a relatively clean phase. Light touch regulation, the non-intrusive trusting approach pioneered by British regulators in the later twentieth and early twenty-first centuries, has been replaced by more intense scrutiny. Structural changes such as the post-Spitzer separation of investor-oriented research from issuer-oriented corporate advice have cleaned up new issues. The dismantling of dedicated proprietary trading units after the US Volcker Rule banned short-term proprietary trading as of 2014 has prevented the most egregious practices of trading on the back of client order flow. Jail time for inside traders and current court cases for some of those involved in benchmark manipulation are likely to have a powerful deterrent effect within the financial community. Proving such actions is difficult, but one barometer is the movement of share prices ahead of takeover deals, which has recently been in decline.

However, it is too early to claim victory in the war against financial corruption. As the veteran British journalist Christopher Fildes has remarked, the time of greatest danger is when the last person to have experienced the previous crisis retires. In an industry in which senior people usually retire in their forties, this creates a very short corridor in which people have firsthand experience of how bad behaviour breaks out and what happens to people and institutions that break the rules. Meanwhile, financial markets are highly skilled at *regulatory arbitrage*, the practice of obeying the letter if not the spirit of the law by means of new techniques to exploit gaps in the rule book.

Let us assume, however, that practitioners are mindful of the rules and are resolved to obey them. Even under those circumstances, the integration of conflicted services into single banks and the complexity of today's deals mean that price-sensitive information is bound to leak. A small army of people is required to make deals happen. A relatively small stock exchange deal in which the author was recently involved had around one hundred people on the approved 'insiders' list. The chances of one of those people inadvertently giving away the secret were high—and so it proved to be as the deal was leaked to the press a few days before it was due to be announced.

In addition, many deals require legitimate market activity ahead of any public announcement, making it possible for seasoned market watchers to work out what is going on. For this reason, the UK's Financial Conduct Authority is probably correct to say that reducing pre-deal suspicious movements to below one case in ten is probably a target that will be beyond the world's financial markets.

And what of the investment banks? A combination of cyclical downturn in market activity and tougher regulations requiring them to hold more capital and curb proprietary trading have led many to trim their business models. There is a new focus on the cost of capital and unproductive assets, and businesses are being shed. This has led some commentators to proclaim the secular decline of the industry, but the investment banks and their hedge fund and private equity cousins retain huge market power and a permissive business model. This advantage seems likely to protect their informational advantage, and *caveat emptor* will remain the best advice their customers can ever receive.

References

Augar, P. 2006. *The Greed Merchants*. London: Penguin.

Stewart, J. 1991. *Den of Thieves*. New York: Simon and Schuster.

12

......

Putting the Lies into Libor:
The Mediation of a Financial Scandal

Peter A. Thompson

With each new legal or technological development, financial market actors have sought to find trading information advantages over their rivals despite regulatory efforts to ensure universal access to market data. Particularly since 'Big Bang' in the City of London (1985–1986) financial institutions have developed increasingly sophisticated new financial instruments to permit the exploitation of narrow price margins in ever-tighter time-frames. In turn, the institutional opacity and technical complexity of these developments has made it more difficult to sustain journalistic scrutiny or regulatory oversight independently of insider sources.

The 2007–2008 sub-prime mortgage crisis and the ensuing 'credit crunch' have raised many questions about the identification and disclosure of financial risks and the capacity of financial analysts and reporters to assess them. Government bank bailouts and subsequent public austerity measures have also generated debate about the relationships that exist between financial markets, their regulators and financial media (e.g., see Schifferes and Roberts 2014; Starkman, 2014; Murdock and Gripsrud 2015).

The extent of the shortcomings of regulators and media in failing to identify the risks of sub-prime mortgage securities have been disputed. Nevertheless, the crisis certainly triggered several regulatory changes and a more critical tone in news reporting of banking. At face value, it might appear that such shifts ought to ensure that future systemic risks to the system are minimised.

However, that may be an over-simplistic reading of the changes that have taken place. Taking the Libor-rigging scandal as a focus, I argue that although some aspects of financial reporting and banking practices have doubtless changed for the better, other structural shortcomings remain largely unaddressed. Understanding the nature of these problems requires consideration of the evolving institutional priorities of the media, financial institutions and regulatory bodies. It also needs recognition that, in many respects, the verification of financial facts and events remains dependent on disclosures from financial regulators and government agencies.

The Libor Scandal

The London Interbank Offered Rate (Libor) is an international benchmark for currency lending and foreign exchange (forex or FX) trading originally developed in the 1980s by the British Bankers Association. The daily rates indicate the level of interest at which banks are able to source loans in different currencies over different periods. The estimated value of contracts and securities underpinned by Libor is somewhere between US$300 and $800 trillion (Wheatley Review 2012). The range of this official estimate reveals just how complex verifying the scale and value of financial securities has become. Libor rates directly influence the daily flows of US$5.3 trillion in forex-related trades, derivatives contracts (FX futures, swaps and options) and bank loans (including mortgages and related securities; BIS 2013).

Until 2014, Libor rates were calculated for ten major currencies across fifteen periods (from overnight to a year, with three-month figures the standard reference). A panel of up to eighteen major banks were asked, 'At what rate could you borrow funds, were you to do so, by asking for and then accepting interbank offers in a reasonable market size just prior to 11 am?' The mean rate was then calculated and published by Thomson Reuters simultaneously across the entire market.

Not well understood outside financial markets, and overshadowed by the wider post-2007/2008 crisis, the revelations of Libor rate manipulation follow a rather uneven timeline (see BBC News 2013). Libor only became a full-blown scandal when it hit the headlines in 2012, following the release of bank communication records revealing collusive activities among the panellist banks. However, misgivings about the validity of the submitted Libor rates had begun to percolate through the financial sector as early as 2005 (see Brummer 2014; Davies 2015). In late 2007, regulators became aware of mass distribution emails expressing suspicions that Libor rates were being routinely under-estimated in case they engendered market perceptions of institutional vulnerability. Interestingly, Barclays (which would soon become the primary focus of the Libor scandal) intimated its own misgivings about Libor rigging to the BBA and the Commodity Futures Trading Commission, albeit without admitting its own complicity (Federal Reserve 2012; FSA 2012; Wheatley

Review 2012). Meanwhile, a Barclays employee also privately communicated concerns to the Fed (Federal Reserve 2012; Milliken and Spicer 2012).

At this time, Libor did begin to receive some attention from the financial media, but the magnitude of the malfeasance underpinning the system was not yet apparent. For example, the ever-prescient Gillian Tett (2007) wrote a *Financial Times* piece noting BBA concerns about Libor mechanisms and rate discrepancies (see Amadeo 2014), and the *Wall Street Journal* carried similar reports (McDonald and MacDonald 2007; Gaffen 2007). In April 2008, the New York Fed Markets Group contacted the Barclays employee who had phoned the group previously. The call confirmed that the banks were worried that high Libor submissions could make an institution appear weak in an environment in which inter-bank credit was quickly evaporating (Federal Reserve 2012). The Fed's subsequent weekly briefing note led to an increase in news reports asking questions about the possibility of Libor manipulation (Federal Reserve 2012).

As the credit crunch deepened in the aftermath of the Lehman brothers collapse in September 2008, valuation models and market liquidity broke down. Crucially, as the crisis deepened and banks stopped lending to each other, the transactions that might have provided an empirical referent for Libor submissions seized up (see Kregel 2012; Thompson 2013; 2015a). As Brummer (2014) notes, the credit crunch led to spreads between banks' actual lending and borrowing rates widening to over one thousand base points, leading the BBA temporarily to suspend publication of the Libor rates (see also Economist 2008). Although not a direct result of the manipulation, Libor had effectively lost any coherent meaning and functionality as a common benchmark. As Mervyn King, the (then) Bank of

England governor, quipped to a Treasury select committee, 'Libor is the rate at which banks don't lend to each other' (quoted in Brummer 2014, 175).

The Trail of Electronic Evidence

As the rumours of rate manipulation spread, the financial media began to pick up the issue and raise more direct questions about the validity of Libor. However, the evidence of collusion stemmed not from investigative news reports but from regulator investigations requiring banks to divulge electronic communication records from financial chat rooms, trading room phone calls and messaging services (see Wheatley Review 2012; Vaughan and Finch 2012; Vögeli and Miller 2015; CFTC 2015b). Although the trail of evidence implicated a wide range of banks, it also pointed to two somewhat different motives behind the Libor manipulation (see Kregel 2012).

First, the reluctance of banks to issue credit to each other led to extreme caution in disclosing any information which might suggest liquidity problems, especially following the collapses of Northern Rock, Bear Stearns and Lehman Brothers (FSA 2012; Federal Reserve 2012). Submitting high rates relative to other banks invited speculation about solvency with potentially self-fulfilling consequences. Comments in exchanges involving Barclays traders reveal the intention was to avoid public speculation about the bank's liquidity. For example: 'Try to get our JPY [Japanese Yen] Libors a little more in line with the rest of the contributors, or else the rumours will start flying about Barclays needing money because its Libors are so high' (quoted in FSA 2012, 25) and 'going 4.98 for Libor only because of the reputational risk . . . basically the[re] is no money out there' (also quoted in FSA 2012, 25).

Second, on a micro-institutional level, the 'Chinese walls' between trading desks and the bank officials responsible for submitting the Libor estimates were evidently porous. Although rate adjustments appeared small, they were significant for forex and interest rate traders, who depended on exploiting small margins or spreads through leverage. Taking the Wheatley Review's lower estimate of Libor-dependent securities of US$300 trillion, even a single base-point shift up or down in the rate could potentially make a difference of US$30 billion to forex trading positions over a year (or US$82.2 million per day). Given that many traders' bonuses are performance-based, the incentive for illicit collusion for personal and institutional gain becomes apparent.

Although senior management typically denied direct knowledge of the micro-level interactions between individual traders, it is implausible that they were unaware of the institutional pressure to avoid signs of vulnerability in the crisis aftermath. The electronic paper trail also suggests an awareness that practices violated regulations and subterfuge was expected. For example: 'Careful how we speak with them about what we, how the rate is set' (RBS trader, quoted in Vaughan and Finch 2012) and 'don't talk about it too much . . . the trick is you do not do this alone . . . this is between you and me but really don't tell ANYBODY' (Barclays trader to external counterparty, quoted in Slater and Ridley 2012).

Other electronic messages suggest Libor manipulation had become widely tolerated as routine practice within some institutions: 'Could we pl[ease] have a low 6mth fix today old bean?' (Deutsche Bank trader, quoted in FCA 2015, 3); 'Look I appreciate the business and the calls we should try to share info where possible also let me know if you need fixes one way or the other' (unidentified FX trader, quoted in CFTC 2015b, 6); 'Dude, I owe you big time! Come over one day after work and I'm opening a bottle of Bollinger' (email to a Barclays banker, quoted in Slater and Ridley 2012).

The Legal and Regulatory Response to Libor Manipulation

The Libor investigations led to a series of formal proceedings and sanctions against the banks. It also became clear that effective manipulation of the rates required collusion across multiple institutions. Although Barclays was the first bank to come to the attention of financial regulators, eight banks have now been fined by UK and US regulators for a total of around US$9 billion. These include Deutsche Bank ($2.5 billion), UBS ($1.5 billion), Rabobank ($1.1 billion), RBS ($612 million), Barclays ($451 million), Lloyds ($383 million), ICAP ($88 million) and RP Martin ($2.3 million; Vögeli and Miller 2015). 2015 also saw the first UK jail sentence imposed on former UBS and Citigroup trader Tom Haynes.

Although these fines are doubtless substantial, they are only a fraction of the banks' annual profits, and banks actively negotiated with regulators over the amounts to be paid to settle the matter (Vögeli and Miller 2015). Recently, US courts have also ruled out claims against banks for Libor manipulation (Van Voris 2015). Consequently, some critics have interpreted the settlements as unduly cosy and suggested links among the 'revolving door' relation between industry and regulators and the lack of court prosecutions and custodial sentences (e.g., Willett 2013).

It is important, however, to note that the BBA Libor system was based not on statutory law, but on a self-regulated market system. Proving that crimes were committed is therefore more complex than simply demonstrating that the Libor mechanism was being gamed. It is intrinsically difficult to calculate specific gains and losses in relation to any individual Libor submission or, indeed, to apportion blame to any specific person or institution. There are many other variables influencing FX-related asset values. A short-term nudge of a few base points on a specific currency on any particular day would benefit as many investors as it harmed. Similarly, while Libor manipulation technically affected hundreds of trillions of dollars' worth of assets, the material impact on the general public should not be overstated. Libor was a public scandal, but the parties most affected were large financial institutions.

A further complication in the Libor scandal was the question of regulator and government complicity with the Libor manipulations at the height of the 2007–2008 crises. In the July 2012 Treasury Select Committee on Libor, Bob Diamond (the recently departed CEO of Barclays) revealed that a few weeks after the collapse of Lehman in September 2008, the deputy governor at the Bank of England (BoE), Paul Tucker, had called Diamond to signal that senior government officials had concerns about Barclays Libor submissions, which were consistently higher than other UK banks. According to Diamond: 'Mr. Tucker stated the levels of calls he was receiving from Whitehall were senior and that, while he was certain that we did not need advice, that it did not always need to be the case that we appeared as high as we have recently' (quoted in BBC News 2012b; see also BBC News 2012a, 2012c).

Diamond discussed the call with Jerry Del Missier, Barclays' chief operating officer, who informed the select committee that he understood this to be an instruction to bring Barclays'

Libor rates down in line with other banks. Tucker, meanwhile, acknowledged that a cabinet secretary and Treasury official had discussed Libor rates with him, but strenuously denied that his conversation with Diamond could be construed as an instruction to rig Barclays' submissions (BBC 2012c; see also Brummer 2014).

The evidence led to speculation that senior government officials regarded Barclays as potentially vulnerable and were willing to overlook discrepancies in Libor reporting with the goal of stabilising the sector. It certainly seems implausible that the BoE and government knew nothing of this until 2012. However, there is no evidence to support more conspiratorial claims that either knew about the level of collusion that preceded the crisis (Kregel 2012). The call to Diamond was perhaps better explained by Barclays' continuing reluctance to accept government credit extended to stabilise the banks rather than any complicity with rigging Libor (Kregel 2012). Nevertheless, insofar as the BBA, FSA and BoE were aware of possible discrepancies with Libor from at least 2007, questions remain about why it took until 2012 for the full story to be uncovered. As Brummer observes, 'No-one thought to look under the bonnet to see just what was going on' (2014, 176).

The accumulation of communications records proving the extent of malfeasance led the Financial Services Authority to recommend an overhaul of the BBA-run Libor model (Wheatley Review 2012). The call made for a new system to be put out to tender, which was won by the Intercontinental Exchange (ICE) Benchmark Administration. ICE Libor now covers a smaller range of currencies, and although it still relies on responses from a panel of banks responding to the same question about borrowing rates, submissions must now reflect actual transactions, with legal prohibitions on making false claims. Moreover, the news model delays the publication of individual bank submissions to offset the risk of inviting speculation about liquidity. Thomson Reuters also ceased to be the collator and publisher of the Libor rates.

Mediation Issues and the Aftermath of Libor

Given that the evidence about Libor manipulation began to emerge in the midst of arguably the most serious systemic financial crisis since 1929, the delays in investigation and resolution are perhaps understandable. The banks responsible have been sanctioned, and the shift to ICE Libor was a significant reform. Indeed, the FSA has itself been restructured into the Prudential Regulation Authority and Financial Conduct Authority (overseen by the BoE's Financial Policy Committee), which are intended to render financial activities more transparent and prevent recurrences of such collusion and manipulation.

The media coverage of the financial crisis and Libor scandal evidenced a willingness to be critical of the financial sector (banks in particular) and avoid financial elite capture (see Picard, Selva, and Bironzo 2014). The fact that Libor became a public scandal and that the reforms to the system have been pushed through is in large part attributable to the news media. However, the key revelations of inter-bank collusion still relied on disclosures from regulatory investigations. This suggests that financial media remained dependent on elite sources for information about internal market processes.

Such limitations do not stem primarily from a lack of journalistic endeavour. Financial events are not publicly accessible in the same way that, say, a public protest or a natural disaster would be. They are ontologically embedded in networks of shared meanings and information flows to which only market participants have direct access. Libor rates themselves are an epistemic construct derived from the metrics and methods of calculation. Ironically, their truth value depends not only on whether the panellist banks submit honest estimates but on whether the rates are collectively recognised as valid by the market as a whole. Although some journalists could discern problems with Libor from the anomalous spreads in the published data, the underlying causes of those anomalies were not apparent to them. The networks of information exchange that underpin professional financial market activity are not usually accessible to outsiders (see Thompson 2013; Davis 2015).

However, it would be premature to suppose that the Libor reforms (and those from the more recent FX fixing scandal), combined with a more critical media, will prevent a recurrence of such problems. The author's recent interviews with both financial wire service editors/reporters and investment bank traders/executives in the City of London (in 2014) suggest a shift in the relations between news media and the banking sector. Now keen to minimise the risk of further reputational damage and regulator scrutiny, investment banks have introduced new restrictions on both internal and external communications. Internally, trading room protocols now routinely record all communications and regulate interactions with counterparties in other institutions. In some cases, personal cell phones and social media have been prohibited. These measures are understandable, but it remains unclear how this would affect the kind of informal communications that arise among traders in crisis scenarios when benchmarks like Libor break down and price activity cannot be discerned from brokerage screens (see Thompson 2015a, 2015b). Thus there are concerns that the new rules restrict entirely legitimate trading room communications. Some representative comments from interviews with senior investment bankers include the following: 'In terms of observations and exchange of information, that's one of the things that the regulatory regime now has, actually in terms of unintended consequences, nobody will share information with you any more'; 'One of the customers made some comments about them checking pricing with other customers about what the other banks were offering. If the banks did that it would be called collusion or rigging the market. If I ring up [other banks named] and say "hey, how are you pricing [company name]?" and that's recorded, that's collusion.'

Meanwhile, in regard to bank interactions with the news media, there has been a significant reinforcement of gatekeeping protocols to manage who responds to journalistic enquiries. The referral of reporters to PR departments and communications managers is far from new, but the tighter rules make navigating these channels more complicated and serve to restrict access to traders at the coalface, as these comments from wire service reporters suggest: 'Access to traders, decision-makers, deal-makers on the floor have become much, much more difficult, for a whole host of reasons. Obviously all the banks and institutions have tightened up massively on who they allow to speak to the press freely'; 'There was a time, eight to ten years ago, where you would ring up the internal communications person and say can I talk to x y or z. Now they want to be in on the call and they will intervene if there's a question asked that's sensitive and they demand checking of quotes afterwards.'

Conclusion

There is no question that the Libor scandal revealed widespread unethical practices, although it is important to differentiate between cases in which reputational damage control was the motive and those driven by personal greed. Many bankers have become wary of what they regard as relentless and (in some cases) unfair media criticism, although one might argue that the banking sector has invited this upon itself.

The more complex question is whether the measures introduced to prevent recurrences of such malfeasance have adequately recognised the constructed nature of metrics such as Libor. The new communication restrictions will arguably make it more difficult for traders to validate price action in a crisis scenario when the shared confidence in benchmarks like Libor break down (especially given that ICE Libor is now based on the very transactional data that dried up at the height of the credit crunch). Meanwhile, journalists may find it more difficult to access the financial sources that have direct experience of the events being reported. As with so many responses to financial crises and scandals, the solutions may inadvertently carry the seeds of future problems.

References

Amadeo, K. 2016. "LIBOR vs. Fed Funds Rate Histories: How the Rate Banks Charge Each Other Warns of Crisis." The Balance, August 13. https://www.the balance.com/libor-rate-historycompare- to-the-fed-funds-rate-history-3306123.

BBC News. 2012a. "Barclays: FSA Regulator Criticises 'Culture of Gaming.'" BBC, July 16. http://www.bbc.com/news/business-18854193.

BBC News. 2012b. "Barclays Reveals Bank of England Libor Phone Call Details." BBC, July 3. http://www.bbc.com/news/business-18695181.

BBC News. 2012c. "Libor Scandal: Paul Tucker denies 'Leaning On' Barclays." BBC, July 9. http://www.bbc.com/news/business-18773498.

BBC News. 2013. "Timeline: Libor-Fixing Scandal." BBC, February 6. http://www.bbc.com/news/business-18671255.

BIS (Bank of International Settlements). 2013. "Triennial Central Bank Survey: Foreign Exchange Turnover in April 2013: Preliminary Global Results." BIS Monetary & Economic Department, September. http://www.bis.org/publ/rpfx13fx.pdf.

Brummer, A. 2014. *Bad Banks: Greed, Incompetence and the Next Global Crisis*. London: Random House.

CFTC (Commodity Futures Trading Commission). 2015a. "Examples of Misconduct in Private Chat Rooms." CFTC Office of Public Affairs. http://www.cftc.gov/idc/groups/public/@newsroom/documents/file/hsbcmisconduct111114.pdf.

Davies, A. 2015. "British Bank Body Was Warned of Distorted Libor As Early As 2005, Court Told." Thomson Reuters, June 8. http://www.reuters.com/article/trial-libor-bba-idUSL5N0YU3Z620150608 .

Davis, A. 2015. "Financial Insider Talk in the City of London." In *Money Talks: Media, Markets, Crisis*, edited by G. Murdock and J. Gripsrud, 29–44. Bristol: Intellect Books.

Economist. 2008. "Banker's Trust." *Economist*, April 24. http://www.economist.com/node/11088888.

FCA (Financial Conduct Authority). 2015. "Final Notice to Deutsche Bank." FCA Ref 150018. https://www.fca.org.uk/publication/final-notices/deutsche-bank-ag-2015.pdf.

Federal Reserve (NY). 2012. "New York Fed Responds to Congressional Request for Information on Barclays-Libor Matter." July 13. https://www.newyorkfed.org/newsevents/news/markets/2012/Barclays_LIBOR_Matter.html.

Foxman, S. 2012. "The NY Fed Says It Noticed Libor Accuracy Problems by Fall 2007." *Business Insider*, July 13. http://www.businessinsider.com/the-ny-fed-just-dumped-all-this-info-about-the-libor-scandal-noticed-libor-accuracy-problems-by-fall-2007-2012-7.

FSA (Financial Services Authority). 2012. "Final Notice to Barclays Bank Plc." FSA Ref 122702, June 27.

Gaffen, D. 2007. "The Meaning of Libor." *Wall Street Journal*, September 7. http://blogs.wsj.com/marketbeat/2007/09/07/the-meaning-of-libor/.

Kregel, J. 2012. "The Libor Scandal: The Fix Is In—the Bank of England Did It!" Levy Economics Institute, September. http://www.levyinstitute.org/pubs/pn_12_09.pdf.

McDonald, I., and A. MacDonald. 2007. "Why Libor Defies Gravity." *Wall Street Journal*, September 5. http://www.wsj.com/articles/SB11889177443 5316875.

Milliken, D., and J. Spicer. 2012. "Barclays Flagged Libor Problem to Fed in 2007." Thomson Reuters, July 16. http://www.reuters.com/article/2012/07/16/us-banking-libor-idUSBRE8680DR20120716.

Murdock, G., and J. Gripsrud, eds. 2015. *Money Talks: Media, Markets, Crisis*. Bristol: Intellect Books.

Picard, R. G., M. Selva, and D. Bironzo. 2014. "Media Coverage of Banking and Financial News." Report for the Reuters Institute for the Study of Journalism, Oxford. http://reutersinstitute.politics.ox.ac.uk/sites/default/files/Media%20 Coverage%20of%20Banking%20and%20Financial%20News_0.pdf.

Schifferes, S., and R. Roberts, eds. 2015. *The Media and Financial Crises: Historical and Comparative Perspectives*. London: Routledge.

Slater, S., and K. Ridley. 2012. "'Done . . . for You Big Boy'—How Emails Nailed Barclays." Thomson Reuters, June 27. http://www.reuters.com/article/2012/06/27/barclays-libor-emails-idUSL6E8HRFL020120627.

Starkman, D. 2014. *The Watchdog That Didn't Bark: The Financial Crisis and the Disappearance of Investigative Journalism*. New York: Columbia University Press.

Tett, G. 2007. "Libor's Value Is Called into Question." *Financial Times*, September 25. http://www.ft.com/cms/s/0/8c7dd45e-6b9c-11dc-863b-0000779fd2ac.html#axzz3t8L4j1sC.

Thompson, P. A. 2013. "Communication and Financial Crisis: Reflexivity and Representation." In *Media Discourses about Crisis*, edited by V. Marinescu and S. Branea, 56–80. Bucharest: Editura Universitatii din Bucuresti.

Thompson, P. A. 2015a. "The Mediation of Financial Information Flows: Traders, Analysts, Journalists." In *The Media and Financial Crises: Historical and Comparative Perspectives*, edited by S. Schifferes and R. Roberts, 169–186. London: Routledge.

Thompson, P. A. 2015b. "Funny in a Rich Man's World: The Contradictory Conceptions of Money in Forex Trading." In *Money Talks: Media, Markets, Crisis*, edited by G. Murdock and J. Gripsrud, 45–64. Bristol: Intellect Books.

Van Voris, B. 2015. "BofA, Barclays Win Narrowing of 27 Libor-Rigging Lawsuits." Bloomberg, August 4. http://www.bloomberg.com/news/ articles/2015-08-04/bofa-barclays-win-narrowing-of-lawsuits-claiming -libor-rigging.

Vaughan, L., and G. Finch. 2012. "Secret Libor Transcripts Expose Trader Rate-Manipulation." Bloomberg, December 12. http://www.bloomberg.com/news/ articles/2012-12-13/rigged-libor-with-police-nearby-shows-flaw-of -light-touch.

Vögeli, J., and H. Miller. 2015. "Deutsche Bank Libor Damage Goes Beyond Record $2.5 Billion Fine." Bloomberg, April 23. http://www.bloomberg.com/ news/articles/2015-04-23/deutsche-bank-libor-damage-goes-beyond-record -2-5-billion-fine.

Wheatley Review. 2012. *The Wheatley Review of LIBOR: Final Report*. UK Treasury, London. https://www.gov.uk/government/uploads/system/ uploads/attachment_data/file/191762/wheatley_review_libor_finalreport _280912.pdf.

Willett, B. 2013. "Central Banks Rigging the Market: Regulators Blind to Libor Fraud." Market Oracle, February 8. http://www.marketoracle.co.uk/Article 38905.html.

13

The Press, Market Ideologies and the Irish Housing Crash

Henry Silke

There is a growing symbiotic relationship between big business, communication networks and the mass media. Business depends on communication networks and the mass media in numerous ways; in the actual conduct of business, in the need for market information, for advertising and market creation and as ideological apparatuses that act to naturalise market economies and defend business interests. Such trends have been exacerbated in the media industry in recent decades as media has been increasingly consolidated into massive transnational corporations with interests far wider than journalism. In fact, it is argued that the contemporary mass media, rather than simply reporting on economic issues, have become an integral part of economic processes.

A clear example of this and of the growing links between business and journalism is the coverage of housing and the property market in Ireland. In 2007/2008 the Irish property market suffered one of the greatest crashes in modern history, eventually costing the state tens of billions of Euros in bank bailouts and hundreds of thousands of mainly working class livelihoods. A key discursive element of housing and property news has been the framing of housing as a commodity rather than a social need, as well as a privileging of market needs over society ones. This was the case in much of the coverage of the housing market by the Irish media in the run up to the housing crash of 2007/2008. This framing, as well as ignoring key social problems such as affordability, included an insidious and dogmatic belief in the primacy of the market that blinded much of the Irish media to the possibility of the crash, thus acting both to encourage and elongate the bubble. There is little evidence that this framing of housing as a commodity rather than a social need has changed; most discourse continues to be around 'fixing the market' rather than thinking outside of it.

The Irish Housing Crisis

The roots of Ireland's economic crisis are long and deep. Ireland after independence remained a dependent economy, concentrating on the export of non-value-added commodities and the enticement of foreign direct investment into the Irish state, rather than the development of indigenous industry. The service economy and the various sections of the property industry became key, state-supported investment activities during the 'Celtic Tiger's' boom years. This led to serious repercussions for many Irish people struggling with a diminishing social housing supply, a Dickensian private rental market and now unaffordable homes. The process also led to a skewed domestic economy and eventually to the development of a massive asset price bubble in property.

By 2007, even middle-class home buyers were being priced out of the housing market. The deregulated banking system filled the gap with innovative 'products' such as speculative '100 percent loans', 'interest-free mortgages' and 'buy to let' schemes. At the same time that consumer demand was dipping, huge amounts of vacant and half-finished properties were coming on stream, often in places with no manifest demand for housing at all. Like all Ponzi schemes (which the Irish property market had begun to resemble), the market was fictitious. Eventually in 2007, property prices began to dip. Following the 'credit crunch' the residential and commercial property markets collapsed entirely. This then uncovered huge holes in banking balance sheets, none larger than those for the poster boy for Irish 'entrepreneurship' and 'innovation', Anglo Irish Bank. However, unlike an ordinary Ponzi scheme, this crash brought down a whole generation of home buyers, the Irish economy, hundreds of thousands of jobs and the living standards of most of the populace.

The crisis in housing has continued since, despite the apparent upturn in the Irish economy. Thousands of people continue to be unable to pay mortgages, often trapped in negative equity (Finfacts Ireland 2013). Public and private investment in new housing remains low (O'Brien 2014b). Private rents continue to rise well above those of inflation or average incomes, especially in Dublin. Unsurprisingly, by the middle of this decade, the city witnessed an unprecedented wave of evictions of individuals and families unable to pay, and we have witnessed what has been termed a 'tsunami of homelessness' (O'Brien 2014a; Kelly 2014).

The Irish Business-Media Nexus

The Irish media sphere is becoming increasingly linked to international investor and political interests. Three distinct trends have developed fairly recently: The first is the consolidation and concentration of Irish media groups; second is increased foreign ownership and penetration; and third is journalistic practice affected by technological change (Horgan, McNamara, and O'Sullivan 2007, 35). The prominent broadcaster RTE, although state-funded, is also dependent on advertising revenue. Within the print media sector, the multinational Independent News and Media (INM) group has developed a dominant position. Its interests range across Irish national, evening and Sunday titles, as well as across the regional market. INM titles represent over 40 percent of all daily and Sunday national newspaper sales in Ireland (Flynn 2013). The company is currently attempting to take over the Celtic Media group, which if successful will mean INM have control of no less than twenty-eight regional titles (National Union of Journalists 2016).

However, the connections between Irish news media and business—most particularly finance—are widespread and entrenched, as a study of Irish director and board networks (2005–2007) has shown (Clancy, O'Connor, and Dillon 2010). Through this network, Independent News and Media directly interlocks with Allied Irish bank, Eircom and other interests. Indirectly, this 'director network' places INM close to the heart of Irish capitalism, which raises the question of absolute neutrality or objectivity in reporting on the Irish economic crisis. Moreover, INM's major shareholder, Denis O'Brien, has huge interests in Irish private radio and international telecommunications, as well as an overly close relationship with Ireland's ministry of communications (Irish Times 2011). His radio holdings include two national radio stations, one of which, *Newstalk*, supplies news to the UTV group of radio stations.

RTE also has connections with the financial oligarchy such as former RTE chairman Patrick J. Wright (who was also a director of Anglo Irish Bank throughout the boom years), and Mary Finan (who was a director of the ICS building society). Although Ireland's 'newspaper of record', the *Irish Times*, is a trust, it too has connections with finance capital. For example, David Went, the former chairman of its board of trustees (2007–2014), has also been chairman of Irish Life and Permanent, chief executive of Ulster Bank and a non-executive director of Goldman Sachs (Mercille, 2013b).

The Irish News Media and the Property Crisis

The Irish media system, especially the press, played an important role in the Irish property bubble and following crisis. Newspapers are one of the main sources of market information and act as the main advertising source for property companies. Newspaper groups have also adapted to the online advertising challenge by using their websites as portals in property listings (e.g., the *Sunday Business Post* and the *Independent*) or even by buying up property websites. The *Irish Times*, for example, purchased www.myhome.ie in 2007 for €50 million (RTE 2007). Newspapers are also an important source of information on the property market, property sales and planning issues.

Although there is some evidence that some minor elements of the news media did ask questions about the property bubble, the wider evidence suggests they most often took a cheerleading role. RTE, the Irish public service channel (and arguably the only media company not overly dependent on property advertising), did belatedly produce a documentary on the possibilities of a housing crash (RTE/Animo Productions 2007). One important article was published as an opinion piece in the *Irish Times* in December 2006, written by the academic Morgan Kelly (Kelly 2006a). The op-ed piece, and the academic paper it drew from (Kelly 2006b), did warn in no uncertain terms of the oncoming crisis.

Newspapers and editors have also defended their roles. For example, former editor of the Irish *Independent* Gerry O'Regan maintained in his evidence, to a government tribunal on the banking crisis, that there was no 'hidden agenda' to 'artificially bolster the property market', while former *Irish Times* editor Geraldine Kennedy claimed that the property sections in the newspapers maintained the same level of editorial standards as were applied to the rest of the paper (TheJournal.ie 2015). Tim Vaughan, former editor of the *Irish Examiner*, stated: "'If we were guilty of anything, and I believe we were, it is that we believed and accepted that institutions, such as the financial regulatory authorities, were doing their jobs and doing them competently with due diligence and with appropriate compliance policies, and with proper political and departmental oversight'" (Hilliard 2015).

At the same time, the RTE documentary and Kelly pieces were widely derided across the Irish press (O'Donoghue 2007). The Taoiseach himself infamously made clear his sentiments towards those who 'talk down the economy' in a public speech (Finfacts Ireland 2007), declaring, 'Sitting on the sidelines, cribbing and moaning is a lost opportunity. I don't know how people who engage in that don't commit suicide'. Alongside its documentary, RTE also produced a reality TV series in which an estate agent turned presenter shamed the populace into the property ladder, in the insidiously named *I'm an Adult, Get Me Out of Here!* (RTE/Animo Productions 2007). RTE also produced and broadcast standard property improvement reality television shows and more recently began running a 'property porn' series entitled *Home of the Year*, sponsored by the Permanent TSB bank (RTE 2015).

Thus far, there has been little discussion about the news media's role in the property bubble in the Irish mass media itself. The media did get a dishonourable mention in the 2011 Nyberg Irish state report on the Irish housing crash (Nyberg 2011, ii, 6, 50). The media's role is also being investigated by the state inquiry into the banking crisis (see Critical Media Review 2015 for video of inquiry proceedings).

In addition, there is a small but growing area of academic research into the role of the media in the Irish economic crisis (Fahy, O'Brien, and Poti 2010; Cawley 2010; Preston and Silke 2011, 2014; Mercille, 2013a, 2013b, 2014). Cawley's (2010) study found that news coverage framed the public sector as a cost while presenting the market economy as the sole 'reality'. Preston and Silke (2014) argued that the media took part in an ideological re-framing of what was a private banking crisis into a fiscal crisis, which then helped lay the political justification for severe austerity measures (see also Mercille 2013a). Mercille (2013b, 2014) found a hugely favourable view of the property market before 2008, which helped sustain the rise in house prices. Some of my own PhD research, on financial journalism and the housing crash between 2007 and 2009, supports these studies and is discussed ahead (Silke 2015).

The Role of the *Irish Times* and the Irish *Independent* in the Property Bubble

As part of a doctoral thesis, I investigated the *Irish Times'* and the Irish *Independent's* coverage of issues around housing and property between May 1 and May 25, 2007. This period coincided with the start of the drop in house prices and the May 24 general election. This election was probably the last major opportunity for debate in the 'public sphere' on the property bubble before the crash, and certainly it was the last opportunity for people to vote before the crash. The key search words 'property', 'housing', 'stamp duty', 'rent' and 'mortgage' were used to find

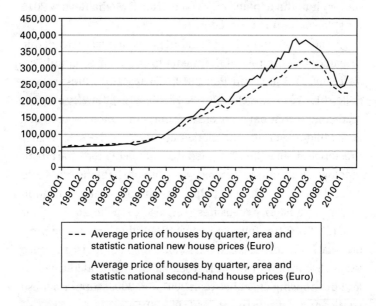

- - - Average price of houses by quarter, area and statistic national new house prices (Euro)

—— Average price of houses by quarter, area and statistic national second-hand house prices (Euro)

Figure 13.1
New and second-hand house prices nationwide, 1990–2010. *Source:* Central Statistics Office.

Table 13.1

Total number of articles featuring property or housing, May 1–25, 2007

	Irish *Independent*	*Irish Times*	Total articles
Residential property	134	124	258
Commercial property	85	66	151
Business and finance	81	104	185
News	106	134	240
Opinion and editorial	4	18	22
Total	410	446	856

articles from the *Irish Times* and the Irish *Independent* in the Lexis Nexis database. Altogether in the *Irish Times*, 446 relevant articles were found between the dates in all four sections; in the Irish *Independent*, 410 relevant articles were found.

As shown in table 13.1, the *Irish Times* and the Irish *Independent* gave approximately equal attention to the issue and generally in the same manner. Most articles in which housing or the property markets were discussed appeared in the property supplements, followed by the news sections, then closely by business sections and finally by opinion and editorial. This in itself suggests that housing is treated as a commodity, being discussed predominantly in the business and advertising sections rather than elsewhere.

In the coverage of property in the *Irish Times* and the Irish *Independent*, a key finding was the dominance of elite sources connected with the property and finance industries as compared to ordinary sources, such as home buyers and renters. The greatest total single overall source on the issue of housing is comprised of estate agents, accounting for some 28 percent of total sources and 29 percent of sources by frequency. In the residential property sections, 64.5 percent of sources in the *Irish*

Times and the Irish *Independent* are estate agents, while in the commercial property sections estate agents make up 72.5 percent of sources in the *Irish Times* and Irish *Independent* combined, 78 percent in the *Irish Times* and 65 percent in the Irish *Independent*. In the combined business sections, banking and finance sources make up 35 percent of sources, while property industry sources (including estate agents) make up 13 percent.

In the news sections, official sources, especially politicians, are most prevalent, with 69 percent of total sources. Seventeen percent of articles also included sources from the finance and property industries. In party political sourcing, the parties with pro-market polices make up the vast majority of sources in the papers, although it may be argued that this reflected party political support at the time. When compared, the Irish *Independent* and the *Irish Times* have a roughly similar ratio of party political representation. Economically right-wing political sources make up the majority, with approximately 65 percent of representatives being openly free market parties (Fianna Fail, Fine Gael and the Progressive Democrats). If we include Labour, which had a 2007 policy of subsidising the market by offering large grants to be used to buy private housing, then the number would go up to approximately 77 percent. Representatives of parties that call for non-market solutions to housing make up just under 9 percent of sources (Sinn Fein, the Socialist Party and People before Profit Alliance), while the Green Party, which called for stricter market regulation, comes in at 10.5 percent. Most party political sources appeared in the news sections.

The most striking figure is that of what we term 'use value' sources—that is, sources such as renters and home buyers who are interested in a property solely for its use (i.e., to live or work in it). 'Use value' sources make up only 2 percent of

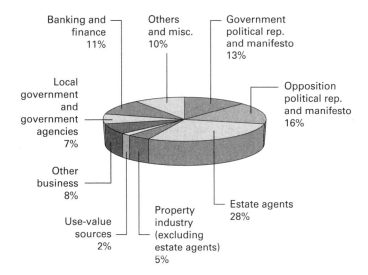

Banking and finance 11%

Others and misc. 10%

Government political rep. and manifesto 13%

Local government and government agencies 7%

Opposition political rep. and manifesto 16%

Other business 8%

Use-value sources 2%

Property industry (excluding estate agents) 5%

Estate agents 28%

Figure 13.2

Total sources from the Irish *Independent* and the *Irish Times* combined.

total sources and appeared in only 2 percent of all articles. In comparison, 'exchange value' sources (from the property and finance industries) make up 43 percent of total sources and appear in 44 percent of all articles.

This overly skewed sourcing could be described as a manifest 'capturing' of the press by property and finance sources and may help to explain the downplaying of the oncoming crisis and the lack of critique of the massive inflation of the cost of housing, as will be discussed ahead.

Treatment and Framing

Research also documented an overall market-orientated frame around property; that is, housing was primarily looked at from the point of view of the market rather than society. Elements of this viewpoint included the privileging of 'exchange value' over 'use value' and non-critical reporting of markets and market sources. For example, although corruption on housing issues such as rezoning was heavily covered in the news sections on the political side, the industrial side of the corruption was completely ignored, and corruption itself was not covered in business or property sections of the papers. Similarly, the state was either presented positively when serving market aims or blamed as a cause of instability in the markets.

The residential property supplement in both newspapers displayed an uncritical, aspirational and advertorial discourse when reporting individual properties. At times, advertorial type articles also find their way into the business and news sections. Not one article questioned whether an individual property might be overpriced. Overall, even in the main news sections, the key issue was 'the market' and 'market stability', rather than either consumer or social good. In the property and commercial sections, the rental property market is framed from the perspective of landlords and investors. Even social housing is framed on a market basis from the point of view of private companies or developers involved in the supply of public housing. In op-ed articles, market stability was the major issue, again trumping the crisis of affordability or the social need for housing. The only questioning of rental prices was from the point of view of business, focusing on the danger of wage demand inflation arising from higher rents.

The discussion of state policy played into the neoliberal trope of state 'interference' distorting a functioning market. Material issues such as overproduction and price inflation were ignored, and assumptions of market self-regulation (without state interference) appeared implied. This is an important finding as it reflected the neo-classical economics viewpoint that markets work and are self-regulating and that the crisis came not from markets themselves but from behavioural, psychological and political interferences. Again, given the non-critical sourcing of both papers from orthodox neo-classical economists and the lack of any evidence of independent fact-checking or investigation, this is probably not surprising.

Both newspapers acted defensively when it came to the question of future property price trends. Both privileged a market slowdown (in positive growth) rather than a crash, with many articles denying that house prices themselves would be affected. The business sections especially acted to play down the dangers of a crash, with some articles even going so far as to attack those who said otherwise.

Many articles considered the problem to be political interference, specifically over stamp duty reform, and expected a post-election 'normality' to resume. This framing held the direct implication that the markets, left to themselves, would be fine, while 'interference' from government and even discussion itself was the problem. This was seen clearly in critical responses to anyone 'talking down the economy'; any critique was itself blamed for causing the crisis. At best, this response ignored the material basis of the property market crisis; at worst, it both silenced critics and elongated the crisis.

Conclusion

Research demonstrates that Irish newspapers covering the property industry did not report objectively or fulfil their public interest 'watchdog' role. Rather, their key function was to act as advertisers for the industry, facilitating exchanges of uncritical information among industry players. In the process, they normalised the hyperinflation of housing, celebrated high property prices and, crucially, acted to play down the contradictions in the Irish system that were directing it towards a crash. With some exceptions, particularly in a few opinion pieces, they reported not for the public but instead for rather narrow sectional and economistic interests. The main reporting patterns and frames point to a 'captured press'—that is, a press in the service of a narrow, elite class-based interest, operating under key structural, institutional and ideological biases.

A key element of this process was the framing of housing not as a social need but as a commodity, used to create wealth rather than supply homes. This celebrated rather than questioned the hyperinflation of housing and rental costs. The market-orientated framing also supported the neo-classical and idealistic belief in market self-regulation, either denying or playing down the possibility of a crash. The lack of critique may well have helped to both build and prolong the bubble itself. That is not to say the media caused the crisis; there were long-term material and political structural issues at its core. However, the newspapers did play the role of facilitator, supplying ideological and political cover to an economic elite that profited greatly from the hyperinflation of housing and the sale of associated financial products. This assisted in laying the grounds for the housing crash, the economic crisis and the subsequent financial bailout, alongside the severe austerity policies that then followed.

References

Cawley, A. 2010. "Sharing the Pain or Shouldering the Burden? News-Media Framing of the Public Sector and the Private Sector in Ireland during the Economic Crisis, 2008–2010." *Journalism Studies* 13 (4): 600–615.

Clancy, P., N. O'Connor, and K. Dillon. *Mapping the Golden Circle*. Dublin: TASC. http://www.tasc.ie/download/pdf/mtgc_may2010.pdf.

Critical Media Review. 2015. "Joint Committee of Inquiry of the Banking Crisis—the Role of the Media." Critical Media Review, March 25. https://criticalmediareview.wordpress.com/2015/03/25/joint-committee-of-inquiry-of-the-banking-crisis-the-role-of-the-media/.

Fahy, D., M. O'Brien, and V. Poti. 2010. "From Boom to Bust: A Post Celtic Tiger Analysis of the Norms, Values and Roles of Irish Financial Journalists." *Irish Communications Review* 12 (1): 5–20.

Finfacts Ireland. 2007. "'Taoiseach Expresses Surprise that 'Cribbing and Moaning' Critics of Irish Economy and Government Policy 'Don't Commit Suicide.'" Finfacts Ireland, July 4. http://www.finfacts.com/irelandbusinessnews/publish/article_1010514.shtml.

Finfacts Ireland. 2013. "Almost 100,000 Irish Residential Mortgages 3 Months in Arrears at End Q2 2013." Finfacts Ireland, August 25. http://www.finfacts.ie/irishfinancenews/article_1026442.shtml.

Flynn, R. 2013. "Media Ownership Concentrated and Under-regulated." *Village Magazine*, May 3. http://villagemagazine.ie/index.php/2013/05/media-ownership-concentrated-and-under-regulated/.

Hilliard, M. 2015. "Financial Information Pointing to Crash 'Inaccessible' to Media," *Irish Times*, March 26. http://www.irishtimes.com/news/politics/financial-information-pointing-to-crash-inaccessible-to-media-1.2153551.

Horgan, J., P. McNamara, and J. O'Sullivan. 2007. "Irish Print and Broadcast Media: The Political, Economic, Journalistic and Professional Context." In *Mapping Irish Media: Critical Explorations*, edited by J. Horgan, B. O'Connor, and H. Sheehan, 33–48. Dublin: University College Dublin Press.

Irish Times. 2011. "Moriarty Says O'Brien Helped Lowry Win Telephone Licence." *Irish Times*, March 3.

Kelly, M. 2006a. "How the Housing Corner Stones of Our Economy Could Go into a Rapid Freefall." *Irish Times*, December 28. http://www.irishtimes.com/business/how-the-housing-corner-stones-of-our-economy-could-gointo-a-rapid-freefall-1.1042463.

Kelly, M. 2006b. "Irish House Prices: Gliding into the Abyss." December 21. http://www.csn.ul.ie/~hugh/att/housing1.pdf.

Kelly, O. 2014. "Over 4,600 Dublin Homeless Seek Emergency Accommodation." *Irish Times*, February 25. http://www.irishtimes.com/news/social-affairs/over-4-600-dublin-homeless-seek-emergency-accommodation-1.1703303.

Kennedy, G. 2015. "Joint Committee of Inquiry into the Banking Crisis." Houses of the Oireachtas, March 26. https://inquiries.oireachtas.ie/banking/wp-content/uploads/2015/03/26032015_GKennedy_vol1.pdf.

Mercille, J. 2013a. "The Role of the Media in Fiscal Consolidation Programmes: The Case of Ireland." *Cambridge Journal of Economics* 38 (2): 281–300.

Mercille, J. 2013b. "The Role of the Media in Sustaining Ireland's Housing Bubble." *New Political Economy* 19 (2): 282–301.

Mercille, J. 2014. *The Political Economy and Media Coverage of the European Economic Crisis: The Case of Ireland*. New York: Routledge.

National Union of Journalists. 2016. "Time to Shout Stop." *Irish Journalist*, October. http://content.yudu.com/web/3pylg/0A3pylh/IJoct16/flash/resources/index.htm?refUrl=https%253A%252F%252Fwww.google.com%252F.

Nyberg, P. 2011. *Misjudging Risk: Causes of the Systemic Banking Crisis in Ireland—Report of the Commission of Investigation into the Banking Sector in Ireland*. Dublin: Government Publications.

O'Brien, C. 2014a. "McVerry Warns of 'Tsunami of Homelessness.'" *Irish Times*, May 18. http://www.irishtimes.com/news/social-affairs/mcverry-warns-of-tsunami-of-homelessness-1.1800268.

O'Brien, C. 2014b. "More than 90% Drop in Social Housing." *Irish Times*, May 6. http://www.irishtimes.com/news/social-affairs/more-than-90-drop-in-social-housing-1.1784594.

O'Donoghue, C. 2007. "Future Shock—Property Crash—the Reaction." *Independent* (Ireland), April 20. http://www.independent.ie/unsorted/property/future-shock-property-crash-the-reaction-26266480.html.

Preston, P., and H. Silke. 2011. "Market 'Realities': De-coding Neoliberal Ideology and Media Discourses." *Australian Journal of Communication* *38 (3)*: 47–64.

Preston, P., and H. Silke. 2014. "Ireland—From Neoliberal Champion to 'the Eye of the Storm.'" *Javnost—The Public* 21 (4): 5–23.

Private Rental Tenancy Board. 2014. "The PRTB Rent Index Quarter 4 2013." http://www.rtb.ie/landlords/rent-index-dec-2014.

RTE. 2015. *Home of the Year*. Television program.

RTE. 2007. "MyHome.ie Sold to Irish Times for €50m." RTE, January 26. http://www.rte.ie/news/business/2006/0728/78794-myhome/.

RTE/Animo Productions. 2007. *I'm an Adult, Get Me Out of Here!* Television program.

Silke, H. 2015. "Ideology, Class, Crisis and Power: The Role of the Print Media in the Representation of Economic Crisis and Political Policy in Ireland (2007–2009)." PhD diss., Dublin City University.

TheJournal.ie. 2015. "Geraldine Kennedy: Charlie Haughey Couldn't Bully Me, so 'Lesser Politicians' Hardly Could." *TheJournal.ie*, March 26. http://www.thejournal.ie/media-banking-inquiry-2014004-Mar2015/.

IV

Private Interest Encroachments
on Public Policy-Making

One of the most disturbing and covert means by which public knowledge is being eroded is in the public policy-making environment, a space often lacking transparency. Not only have private sector companies increasingly taken on state sector roles, through a mixture of privatization and outsourcing, so too have they increasingly taken over the decision-making process itself. Commercial lobbyists, think tanks and consultants provide a stream of reports, data and policy information that feeds into government departments. Legal, accounting and other experts are seconded from the private to the public sector to develop new laws and regulations before returning to exploit such knowledge for their long-term private employers. Everywhere one looks, from defence to health, education to finance, the policy-making process has been captured by vested interests.

In chapter 14, Bong-hyun Lee outlines the ways and means by which chaebols (Korean conglomerates) have taken over multiple forms of public policy-making and discourse about the economy itself. Their dominance has come through strong influence over think tanks, state-centred policy networks, business journalism and public relations units. It is by such means that economic power has shaped discourse, which, in turn, has reshaped the economy in Korea. Consequently, its previous state-sponsored development model has been reconfigured towards a more neoliberal capitalist template, bringing instability and extreme inequalities along the way.

In chapter 15, Michael Moran and Karel Williams take a close look at the growing outsourcing industry—another means by which the private sector encroaches on the state. They ask: Why does outsourcing continue to expand despite ongoing fiascos, frauds and cost over-runs? Answers lie somewhere between public and institutional financial illiteracy, market ideology and sleight-of-hand public discourses. The combination means that outsourcers keep profiting and growing—and at a cost to the public purse.

In chapter 16, Janine Wedel takes a close look at the new American influence elites, their modes of operation, and the vehicles and structures they co-create in order to advance their individual agendas. As traditional institutions and hierarchies become more fragmented, so the new breed of influence elites and flexible networks moves in to the policy-making spaces that open up. Such elites have moved far beyond the 'standard revolving door' as they move effortlessly between public legislative and regulatory bodies, private contractors, think tanks, consultancies and media outlets, leveraging inside knowledge and contacts as they go. Ultimately, these same elites have powerful input into numerous policy-making areas, from defence decisions and contracts to financial regulation. Their personal gain is often the public's loss.

In chapter 17, Colin Leys outlines a major shift in the way UK health care policy is constructed. Starting in the 1920s, health care was debated very much within a public sphere made up of the professions, universities, media and government, thus linking policy to the public interest. However, after the late 1970s, this model was slowly dismantled. Instead, management consultancies and privately funded think tanks took over the policy-coordinating function of the Department of Health. It is this transition that has aided the shift towards the privatization and marketization of the National Health Service (NHS).

14

The Corporate Takeover of Economic Discourse in Korea

Bong-hyun Lee

This chapter illustrates how *chaebols*, a type of conglomerate particular to South Korea, have enhanced their influence over government policy via their growing control over multiple forms of public economic discourse. Chaebols have deployed their significant economic resources to strategically dominate both public media and state-generated policy debates about the economy. Their success in this area of public culture has meant that chaebols have a greater say over economic policy than the state itself, which, in turn, has contributed to a significant undermining of the democratic process.

The Role of Chaebols in Korean Economic Growth

Chaebols, such as Samsung, Hyundai and LG, are a specific type of conglomerate most commonly associated with Korea. They developed during the country's period of 'condensed economic growth'. In most of the literature, Korean chaebols are defined by three distinctive characteristics: corporate governance (family ownership and control); market position (monopolistic or oligopolistic); and organizational structure (business groups with multiple ownership and managerial links). These characteristics are very similar to those of the zaibatsu before the defeat of the Japanese empire in 1945.

Chaebols emerged and evolved when the Korean economy surged forward from the mid-1960s onwards. This period of rapid economic growth coincided with a massive consolidation of capital by chaebols, working in tandem with the government as it pursued a state-driven developmental model. In fact, Amsden (1989) attributed the impressive achievements of the Korean model to this evolving state-chaebol partnership.

In this partnership, the state first took the initiative by harnessing institutional support and economic discipline. But by the late 1970s, the state-driven developmental model was reaching its limits. It became increasingly clear that the state no longer dared to orchestrate everything. A new paradigm was evolving to prolong economic development. It was economic globalization, motivated by the 'boundless dynamics of capitalism' (Colás 2005, 73), that supplied the new 'frame of reference' (Said 2003) for this paradigm shift. Liberalism, resuscitated in the face of the 'structural crisis of capitalism' (i.e., the falling rate of profit) in the 1970s, has since appropriated globalization as a means for expanding capitalist activities unchecked across national boundaries. Both transnational corporations (TNCs) and global financial capital have played a pivotal role in making 'the capitalist global system the dominant global system' (Sklair 2002, 7).

Neoliberal ideas and neoliberal policy regimes were voluntarily adopted by the Korean state and by chaebols, replacing the economic ideas of the developmental era. Consequently, the decade-long partnership between the state and the chaebols started to change, with the state no longer acting as the dominant partner.

The chaebols, consistent with their nature as capitalist, monopoly-seeking entities, have pursued freedom and expansion in the course of the neoliberal transformation of Korean society. Once established, they aspired towards greater freedom from state regulation, a restructuring of labour-capital relations, and the marketization of multiple areas of society. Since the early 1980s, they have demanded that the government ease financial regulations so they could access cheaper international sources of capital. By the mid-1990s, through a combination of acquisitions and enhanced access to global capital, they had gained considerable financial autonomy. At this point, they began publicly demanding that the state retreat from the economic sphere (Ha 2003, 10).

The Korean economic crisis in 1997 was a direct consequence of state withdrawal from economic coordination, which included a rapid relaxation of cross-border capital movement controls and the abolition of industrial policy, both without establishing state regulatory systems. Furthermore, the general turn towards neoliberal restructuring (based on IMF programmes) of the Korean economy following the 1997 economic crisis has accelerated the ascendancy of capital over state.

Chaebol Economic Influence Based on Growing News and Information Dominance

Chaebols, with their extensive links to umbrella associations, in-house think tanks and extensive social networks, constitute a most influential site of discursive power in contemporary

Korean society. The contrasting corporate discourses promoted by chaebols set them apart from their conglomerate counterparts in Western economies. On the one hand, they are fairly modern economic institutions, publicly listed transnational companies producing world-class goods and services. On the other hand, they have an oddly pre-modern corporate governance system, which is the legacy of small, start-up family businesses, strongly controlled by all-powerful chairmen's family members, who own tiny proportions of the company's stock. Many of the resources of chaebols—ideas, personnel and money—have been mobilized in order to consolidate this family dominance. In such organizations, fealty to the chairman is as important as ability when it comes to staff promotions.

Many practices, beliefs, discourses and forms of culture arise from this peculiar chaebol-centred system and permeate every corner of Korean society. To create a favourable business environment and to cover over their deficiencies, chaebols deploy extensive resources to manage their political, legal and social environments. They systematically cultivate extensive elite networks of politicians, journalists, lawyers, scholars and artists. They abhor the power of the state, arguing that government regulations suffocate the free market—but their relentless request for deregulation in effect also reflects their desire to prevent state reforms of the archaic chaebol system, which itself inhibits competition.

The social vision of chaebols determines that social advancement is only achieved through economic growth. They present themselves simultaneously as locomotives of growth and as part of a national team in the global economic battle. In this way, the state is relegated to the role of cheerleader for business activities. The political leanings of chaebols are highly conservative, mirroring their authoritarian organizational ethos. Their social vision is too narrow to accept liberal pluralism. Their belief is that all forms of collectivism (e.g., industrial action, political ascendancy of labour groups) and distributive social policies are only hindrances to economic growth.

Communication within chaebol-centred networks is intensive. The senior staff of chaebols and their umbrella associations actively meet various elites (e.g., politicians, government officials, journalists and businessmen) during their lunch or dinner hours. The information garnered from these meetings is not held privately but keyed into the online information archive systems of their companies. This information is later integrated, analysed by specialists and circulated to senior personnel. What's more, many chaebols operate a task force team that is solely dedicated to collecting inside information from various elite networks. Different chaebol task forces then have regular meetings with their counterparts and exchange information.

In this system, some chaebols are said to have greater information-gathering power than the government intelligence agency itself; one famous anecdote relates that Samsung, in 1998, received information about the death of the Chinese leader Deng Xiaoping through its international elite networks several hours before the first world news wire was released. Information, concerns and ideas gathered are widely discussed across chaebol networks, in many cases leading to a rough chaebol-wide consensus. This consensus then provides the rationale for chaebol public arguments or actions, especially when they interact with external elite groups.

Chaebols are very good at managing the media as a means of achieving and sustaining their power in society. Their in-house PR units have considerably augmented their personnel and resources in recent decades. Professional PR is now seen as a critical means of gaining direct or longer-term strategic advantage in business, and chaebol PR departments have become a route for staff to be promoted to the executive level. When a crisis or conflict breaks out, PR personnel are deployed not only to foster favourable public opinion, but also to persuade or dissuade related elite groups.

In ordinary times, however, a more sophisticated and fundamental type of PR is mobilized. The aim of this 'strategic PR' is to spread a business-friendly version of knowledge about specific economic, social and political issues. Many in-house chaebol think tanks or umbrella associations competitively produce issue-related research papers every day. Ironically, in contemporary Korea it is chaebol-affiliated research institutes that engage most actively and in the timeliest way with social and economic issues; many public research institutions are too lacking in resources to offer much. The target of strategic PR is by its nature non-corporate elite groups or opinion leaders. In-house chaebol institutions distribute their research papers through their own email lists. Some of these, usually those dealing with sensitive issues, are only distributed to members of elite groups (e.g., high-ranking government officials or top management) several days before being published more widely. Think tanks generally work in close cooperation with PR departments, and PR departments then promote the research papers when deemed strategically useful; sometimes, they request specific research to advance a PR objective.

Mass news media is closely intertwined with the communication process constructed by chaebols, which are the most important advertisers for newspapers and for broadcasting. Because of worsening financial conditions, quite a lot of media corporations have abandoned the principle of a firewall between their editorial and management departments. At the same time, many media corporations are closely linked to chaebols through their ownership structures. For these reasons, journalists often mobilize self-censorship mechanisms in their reports on chaebol-related issues. Frequently, chaebols' PR personnel directly harass journalists in an attempt to block unfavourable news; in most cases, they are successful.

However, a corporate 'mobilization of bias' comes equally from day-to-day organisational relations, which means that censorship does not have to be directly imposed. Most business journalists are stationed in press rooms that chaebols or their umbrella associations supply. Hovering around the press room, journalists regularly have contact with PR staff or senior managers of chaebol groups during their lunch or dinner hours. From time to time, PR departments organize conferences or tours in which several key managers from chaebol headquarters stay for one night with business journalists, editors or economic columnists. Major chaebol groups even support overseas study programmes for journalists for a year and keep in contact with, for example, their so-called Samsung or LG fellows after they return. In this respect, the level of interaction that business journalists have with chaebol staff is far higher than that with small and medium company managers or the representatives of labour unions. Thus, journalists unknowingly internalize the perspectives and values of chaebols.

The dependency of journalists on chaebol PR departments has grown as media companies have struggled to fill space in an era of declining revenues. Few now have the resources to create an in-depth or investigative piece on a business. Access to senior chaebol personnel is strictly controlled through the PR department. Reliance on chaebol-crafted press releases, think tank reports and comments is widespread. The similar orientations of business journalists to these same chaebol sources then leads to 'pack journalism' in which all news producers follow similar storylines, frames and opinions. In appearance, reporters seem to engage in intense competition, but outcomes seldom vary much.

Chaebols Mobilize Discourse against the Korean State and Society

The exaggeration of bad economic conditions by chaebols and media, with a view to influencing economic policy, has been a recurrent issue since the late 1990s. This argument has appealed directly to individuals while ignoring macro-economic indicators that have continued to show sound growth in the Korean economy. The larger depression discourse has had two socio-political purposes. One was to put pressure on the government to take a more 'business-friendly' stance because 'negative economic conditions' were continually attributed mainly to government regulation and interference in the economy. Thus, the discourse implied that if government and politicians would leave businesses (especially chaebols) to their own courses, the economy would naturally become robust. The other purpose was to argue that 'economic redistribution' was best left to the market and achieved through economic growth. Korea has shown a steady deterioration of income distribution since it began forcefully adopting neoliberal policies after the economic crisis of 1997. The population's sense of economic depression mainly comes from this growing inequality, increasing casualisation of work, the rapid appreciation of asset values, such as real estate, and the ever-increasing expense for private education. However, the discourse of depression only highlighted under-investment, implying that once hesitant chaebols and business leaders were encouraged to invest, then everything would be well.

The power of chaebols to dominate economic discourse became evident in 2003–2004. Chaebols and the mainstream media simultaneously argued that the economic situation was terrible and relentlessly played up a sense of depression, thus forcing the newly inaugurated Roh Moo-Hyun government into a political corner. This took place in spite of the fact that major economic indicators, such as GDP growth, the Industrial Production Index and rises in per-capita income, were all sound and the economy was clearly recovering from its 2001–2002 depression. Once again, deregulation and entrepreneurial inducements were what the government was publicly told it should follow through on.

Conclusion

Bresser Pereira (1984) explored a similar democratisation process in Brazil, whereby the emerging bourgeoisie that grew up dependent on state patronage then developed their own autonomy. As soon as they gained enough power to accumulate capital without state assistance, they then moved to acquire hegemonic power over the state. In contemporary Korean society, very few people would disagree with the argument that the hegemony of chaebols has become firmly established. As the power of the chaebols has grown, they increasingly have undertaken a quasi-state role, expanding to take the place of a retreating state.

In the case of Korea, the culture and communication environments of chaebol-centred networks have become a significant weapon for achieving corporate policy goals. This has had a strong material impact on Korea as the perspectives, voices and strategies of chaebols overwhelm wider society. The voices of labour, reformist civil society groups and small and medium companies are systematically omitted. Within this imbalance of communicative power, chaebols have emerged as the most powerful social group in Korea, the influence of which often appears to surpass that of government. Economic globalization has provided great momentum for chaebols to inflate their social legitimacy and influence on society to the best of their ability. What corporate elites and pro-business experts promote in the era of globalization is a set of seemingly ambivalent ideas and discourses. On the one hand, they postulate that they are ardent supporters of the supremacy of the market. They relentlessly call for the deregulation and retreat of the state in the economic sphere. The idea of *footloose capital* provides their new identity in this era. On the other hand, they portray the globalized world as an economic battlefield among nation states. Evoking nationalistic sentiment, they represent themselves as defenders of the national interest against foreign capital. By juggling these two arguments—globalism and nationalism—what corporate elites garner from society and the state is in fact a *race to the bottom* in order to support *our* corporations.

References

Amsden, A. 1989. *Asia's Next Giant: South Korea and Late Industrialization.* Oxford: Oxford University Press.

Colás, A. 2005. "Neoliberalism, Globalisation and International Relations." In *Neoliberalism: A Critical Reader,* edited by A. Saad-Filho and D. Johnston, 70–80. London: Pluto Press.

Ha, Yeon-Seob. 2003. "Policy Idea and Institutional Change: Translating Neoliberalism in Korea." *Korean Review of Administrative Science* 44 (4): 1–27.

Pereira, L. B. 1984. *Development and Crisis in Brazil: 1930–1983.* Boulder, CO: Westview Press.

Said, E. 2003. *Orientalism.* New York: Random House.

Sklair, L. 2002. *Globalization: Capitalism and Its Alternatives.* 3rd ed. Oxford: Oxford University Press.

15

The Tropes of Unlearning:
UK Responses to Outsourcing Fiascos

Michael Moran and Karel Williams

We have elsewhere described the unlearning state (Bowman et al. 2014) and how liberal democracy in the United Kingdom can, like the restored Bourbons, learn nothing and forget nothing as the nation persists with its unsuccessful thirty-year experiment in competition and markets. Generalisations about neoliberal policy making and austerity politics, or pervasive conditions like the financial illiteracy of electorates, do not entirely explain such unlearning in this kind of polity, which authors like Crouch (2005) describe as *post-democratic*. Here, in various policy areas, the political classes need tropes that both serve as alibis for failure and suggest lessons learned so that everything can carry on much as before—until the next time, when the same tropes will be reused to convey an impression of purposive response to the challenge of events.[1]

We are here dealing with the corruption of liberal democracy, which should have a developed capacity to learn from failure. Liberalism should promote open debate about policy options, their alternatives and their consequences, and democratic institutions should ensure accountability of governments in the face of failure. These safeguards should not be rubbished, because they are worth something. The great domestic policy disasters of the last century—genocides and famines—have occurred in non-democratic regimes and are directly connectable to the institutional and ideological arrangements in those regimes. Liberal democracies have not inflicted suffering on anything like this scale—at least, not on their own citizens. However, liberal democracies are not immune from blindness in the face of failure, and this chapter illustrates this point by considering how the UK political classes respond to fiascos about service delivery, cost over-runs and fraud in outsourced public services.

This case is particularly important for some very obvious reasons. Outsourcing itself is now one of the most important economic and political developments in the United Kingdom of the last three decades, and the practice is now being imitated in many other countries. The scale of the outsourcing boom in the United Kingdom has produced a new industry with £100 billion in turnover and what we have called a 'franchise state'—a configuration in which private outsourcing giants assume responsibilities for core state functions like security and welfare (Bowman et al. 2015).

Failures to prevent recurrent outsourcing fiascos or to learn from them thus constitute major failures of public responsibility—and the failure to learn is, as we explain ahead, tied to a series of tropes or devices that allow the political classes to explain away each new failure as a setback that does not justify halting outsourcing or imposing much tighter conditions on outsourcing contractors. This failure to reflect creatively on the causes of fiascos and how they might be avoided stymies public debate and criticism and undermines the institutions dedicated to public oversight of outsourcing: the National Audit Office and the system of Select Committees in the House of Commons, notably the House of Commons Public Accounts Committee.

Official reports have dissected successive outsourcing fiascos, including fraud over prisoner tagging, failure to provide security guards at the London Olympics and many mundane failures of service delivery on general practitioner out-of-hours services, court translation services and such like. Ahead, we discuss three tropes that stand in the way of governmental learning from such outsourcing fiascos. They are important learning blocks, because they recur with minor variations in different responses to various fiascos and because they are connected to wider features of a policy-making system in which ill-considered hyper-activity produces many other failures. Readers are invited to consider how similar tropes recur in other policy areas in other high-income countries.

Trope 1: 'It'll Be Lovely When It's Finished': The Receding Market Utopia

The oldest joke about Manhattan—'it'll be lovely when it's finished'—also underlies one of the commonest responses to the failures of utopian projects: The problem always lies with the failure to realise in full the underlying conditions needed for the project to succeed. The mindset created by the pursuit of the utopian ideal has been explored in Scott's famous study of human catastrophes inflicted by authoritarian high modernism—the utopian fiascos of, for instance, Stalinist and Maoist utopianism (Scott 1998). Outsourcing in the United Kingdom takes place in a liberal democratic society, but it has the key features of a utopian project; it aims at the fundamental reconstruction of the state according to an imaginary map of an ideal social order— one in which government services are delivered as a result of bidding in a freely competitive market. When the competitive process fails to deliver, the cause is therefore ascribed to the failure to realise the required conditions for reaching the utopian destination, and a further reconstruction of institutions is embarked upon to reach the ever-receding market utopia. For example, the National Audit Office responded in December 2013 to numerous instances of the failure of the outsourcing system to create a defensible system for pricing outsourced services by creating an ideal set of outsourcing principles that need to be put in place for a pricing system to work. We summarize from a longer passage (National Audit Office 2013, 9–19):

Principle one: The relevant department understands national supply and demand and intervenes to remedy problems

Principle two: The relevant department understands the national market structure and intervenes in the event of market failure

Principle three: The relevant department should understand the role of, and work with, the competition authorities and relevant quality and sector regulators, to raise awareness, standards and enforce rules and the right market behaviour

Principle four: The local authority understands its impact on local public and private markets as a purchaser of services, and how to encourage the right market behaviour

Principle five: The local authority knows the costs of service provision

Principle six: The price sustains supply at acceptable levels

Principle seven: Quality is acceptable

Principle eight: Users are well informed about quality

The problem is not that any of these conditions are unacceptable, nor is it the case that they are in some instances not partly realisable (indeed, the NAO's own report cites individual instances in which some institutions have succeeded in putting some of the principles into effect). Instead, they cumulatively amount to a utopian imaginary—a set of conditions that could never in practice be achieved but which can be used to explain why the kind of real live pricing failures that prompted the NAO report can be explained. It is easy to see that the realisation of all these conditions fully and simultaneously is a utopian mirage—but the vision of the mirage can be used to legitimise the continuing pursuit of a society in which government services are outsourced despite the recurrence of fiasco.

Trope 2: 'That's Life': Fatalism

The utopian mirage is one end of the spectrum of responses to failings in the outsourcing system. A very different response at the other end of the spectrum is fatalistic: Quite contrary to the utopian aspiration, it assumes that not only is it impossible to achieve perfection but that failure and fiasco are the normal lot of government—and indeed of life. Utopianism is revolutionary; fatalism is conservative. It is one of the commonest tropes in British government when faced with fiasco (see Moran 1991, 2007). The world is a complicated place. The complexity of life is such that mistakes must always happen. History is lived forward but studied backward. Only smart alec journalists, academics who study things after the event, and Parliamentarians who want to make partisan points at the expense of those who actually have to implement policy think that failures should have been foreseen. In outsourcing, organisations are large and complex; it is practically impossible to control every last operating detail in a giant firm. We learn as best we can from these mistakes, but cannot rule out the possibility of future failure (on the route of our onward march).

In human terms, this is a perfectly understandable response that grows from the lived experience of those who actually have to make the outsourcing system work, because they confront the hard realities of institutional organisation and policy delivery. It is therefore not surprising that fatalism is a common explanation for failure offered by those who actually have to run outsourcing programmes. It is one of the most frequent responses by hapless senior executives of outsourcing companies being roasted for failures before the Public Accounts Committee. Consider as absolutely typical the explanations offered by leading executives for one of the most widely publicised fiascos of recent years: the failure of anyone to spot that two of the outsourcing corporate giants (G4S and Serco) were billing for services (tagging prisoners) that had never been carried out. Ashley Alemanza, chief executive of G4S at the time of the hearings (December 2013), offered the following: 'I think it was a judgment that was flawed. It was just a flawed judgment. . . . We got it wrong. . . . We did not have the systems in place that we needed to have' (House of Commons Public Accounts Committee 2014, Q113, Q116). A similar line was taken by the then chairman of Serco on the same occasion: 'As far as we are concerned (it) might have been a contractual interpretation of what the lawyers might argue, but that still does not make it right' (ibid., Q115).

One reason fatalism is so often invoked in this way is that those at the sharp end of the outsourcing system—executives responsible in the last instance for implementing programmes—are in the first line of criticism when fiascos occur. And they are in the first line because of the third, commonest response to fiasco in the outsourcing system: blame shifting.

Trope 3: 'Whose Fault Is It Anyway?': Blame Shifting

As the work of Hood and his colleagues demonstrates, blame shifting is a standard response to policy failure in British government (Hood 2002; Hood and Rothstein 2001). It is profoundly inimical to efficient policy learning, because it transforms systemic defects into human failings, creating a trail of stigmatised public servants and executives who are publicly scapegoated for failure, either in official reports or (more vehemently) in the tabloid press. The following summary by the Public Accounts Committee of the whole outsourcing experience catches this kind of reasoning in its most sober and balanced form—with a lament for the incapacity of firms and civil servants, which must both do better:

> Government is clearly failing to manage performance across the board, and to achieve the best for citizens out of the contracts into which they have entered. Government needs a far more professional and skilled approach to managing contracts and contractors, and contractors need to demonstrate the high standards of ethics expected in the conduct of public business,

and be more transparent about their performance and costs. The public's trust in outsourcing has been undermined recently by the poor performance . . . high profile failures illustrate contractors' failure to live up to standards expected and have exposed serious weaknesses in Government's capability in negotiating and managing private contracts on behalf of the taxpayer. (House of Commons Public Accounts Committee 2014, 3)

Two particular features of the outsourcing policy system reinforce this propensity towards blame shifting: The first is the historically established system for ensuring accountability, which is built around two institutions—the National Audit Office (a descendant of nineteenth-century institutions concerned with auditing for value for money in public spending) and the system of Select Committees in the House of Commons, which react to NAO reports to hold public hearings and issue their own critical reports. Of these Select Committees, the most important is the Public Accounts Committee, itself a nineteenth-century 'value for money' institution of accounting scrutiny. The incentive structures of parliamentary life encourage the development of an inquisitorial investigative style in which publicity is generated for chairs of the committee and for committee members by aggressive cross-questioning of witnesses and by the publication of reports that equally aggressively criticise the public servants who wrote the original outsourcing contracts and the executives of the companies that tried to put them into effect. The activities of the committee under two particularly successful recent chairs (Edward Leigh, 2001–2010, and Margaret Hodge, 2010–2015) have been shaped to the needs of modern media management: brief, stylised confrontations in committee hearings ideal for news bulletin clips and media interviews with chairs at launches of committee reports to highlight the 'headline' messages of those reports.

A second feature of the outsourcing system reinforces blame shifting. In recent years, outsourcing has moved on from contracting out utility services, like waste management and transport, to contracting out historically core state functions, like the management of security and the management of welfare claimants. These include some of the most sensitive and politically toxic tasks of the state—for instance, incarcerating and sometimes deporting failed asylum seekers and scrutinising welfare claimants for their ability to undertake employment. Although justified in the language of efficiency and competitiveness, outsourcing here involves shifting to the private sector tasks that are so politically toxic that elected politicians would prefer not to manage them. The result is that when things (fairly predictably) go wrong, the blame can be shifted to the outsourcer. In that case, government ministers have two options: (1) they can harrumph about 'completely unacceptable' failures in duty of care in secure institutions; or (2) they can simply let the outsourcers as enforcers take the punishment for operating within what is government policy (but not explicitly so).

The way in which enforcers can be used to take the punishment is nicely illustrated by the series of outsourced contracts connected with work capability assessments (fitness for work assessments for disabled benefit claimants). In March 2014, the Department of Work and Pensions and the outsourcing specialist Atos announced that the contract signed by Atos with the previous Labour government to carry out work capability assessments was to be cancelled a year early. The staff of Atos had been required to make brutal judgements about individual cases; underqualified, time-pressured and poorly incentivised staff made judgements that upended lives and could be challenged. In giving reasons for walking away, Atos explained how, as enforcer, it had taken the punishment: 'The key ones were the very toxic environment in which their staff were being asked to work, including threats and security incidents, the lack of public understanding of the separate roles of Atos, DWP and tribunals in the process, leading to Atos being blamed for withdrawal or refusal of benefit; and the contract becoming less viable financially' (House of Commons Work and Pensions Select Committee 2014, 29).

And this is how government washed its hands of the toxic experience. In the words of the then minister for Disabled People to the Work and Pensions Committee:

> When I arrived in the Department eight months ago, on my desk were an awful lot of letters from my colleagues—let us be perfectly honest about it—from across the House who had real concerns about how the assessments were being done and how Atos was performing . . . it did become pretty obvious that Atos's confidence as to whether they could perform what we were asking them to do; our confidence; and the public's confidence was not sufficient, and so I did ask the team to negotiate with Atos as to whether or not Atos could leave the contract. (House of Commons Work and Pensions Select Committee 2014, Q447)

Blindsided by Tropes: Unlearning and Outsourcing

Although blame shifting is the most common response to the outsourcing fiasco, the most important source of knowledge blockage is the utopianism identified earlier; for nearly three decades now, the management of contracting has been in thrall to an ideological vision for competition and markets. The failures in the ramshackle outsourcing system have been nowhere near as catastrophic as those in the old command systems that were guided by authoritarian collectivist ideologies. However, the inability to learn from failure is strikingly similar. It is hardly surprising that Ron Amman, who spent the first part of his career studying the pathologies of the Soviet command system and the second as a senior manager in the British policy system, ended up finding strong similarities between the two (Amman 2003).

Note

1. This chapter draws on our recent book (Bowman et al. 2015), which presents a broader overview of outsourcing that combines follow the money research and political analysis.

References

Amman, R. 2003. "A Sovietological View of Modern Britain." *Political Quarterly* 74 (4): 468–480.

Bowman, A., I. Ertürk, P. Folkman, J. Froud, C. Haslam, S. Johal, A. Leaver, M. Moran, N. Tsitsianis, and K. Williams. 2015. *What a Waste: Outsourcing and How It Goes Wrong*. Manchester, UK: Manchester University Press.

Bowman, A., I. Ertürk, J. Froud, S. Johal, J. Law, A. Leaver, M. Moran, and K. Williams. 2014. *The End of the Experiment: Outsourcing and How It Goes Wrong.* Manchester, UK: Manchester University Press.

Crouch, C. 2005. *Post-democracy.* Cambridge: Polity Press.

Hood, C. 2002. "The Risk Game and the Blame Game." *Government and Opposition* 37 (1): 15–37.

Hood, C., and H. Rothstein. 2001. "Risk Regulation under Pressure: Problem Solving or Blame Shifting?" *Administration & Society* 33 (1): 21–53.

House of Commons Public Accounts Committee. 2014. *Contracting Out Public Services to the Private Sector. Session 2013–14. HC 777.* London: The Stationery Office.

House of Commons Work and Pensions Select Committee. 2014. *Employment and Support Allowance and Work Capability Assessments. Session 2014–15. HC 302.* London: The Stationery Office.

Moran, M. 1991. "Not Steering but Drowning: Policy Catastrophes and the Regulatory State." *Political Quarterly* 72 (4): 414–427.

Moran, M. 2007. *The British Regulatory State: High Modernism and Hyper-innovation.* Oxford: Oxford University Press.

National Audit Office. 2013. *Deciding Prices in Public Services Markets: Principles for Value for Money.* London: National Audit Office.

Scott, J. 1998. *Seeing like a State: How Certain Schemes to Improve the Human Condition Have Failed.* New Haven, CT: Yale University Press.

16

Meet the New American Influence Elites: How Top Players Sway Policy and Governing in the Twenty-First Century

Janine R. Wedel

A new breed of influence elites has emerged in recent years, spawned by a sea change over the past several decades. As a social anthropologist, I have been mapping these elites' modus operandi and organisation and the vehicles they set up to help organize their influence. These novel elites follow a twenty-first-century playbook, holding sway through flexible and often informal means; they are less stable, more mobile, more global and less visible than their forebears of living memory. And, as I demonstrate in *Unaccountable: How the Establishment Corrupted Our Finances, Freedom and Politics and Created an Outsider Class*, they largely defy democratic oversight. Yet these players and their practices are systemic in the United States, in arenas ranging from finance and military policy to energy and health care.

Understanding how American influence elites operate is crucial because their practices are far-reaching and they influence decisions that affect the entire world. Because these elites appear to have played a role in widening inequality and also because they have morphed beyond conventional concepts that explain their influence—lobbies, revolving doors, interest groups, and 'kitchen cabinets'—it is all the more urgent to explicate their modus operandi, organisation and impact.

From Power Elites to Influence Elites

The way elites organize influence today—their modus operandi and organisation—differs from the methods of 'power elites' as described by sociologist C. Wright Mills sixty years ago (Mills 1956). Mills famously coined the term *power elite* to describe the interlocking constellation of government officials, military leaders and corporate executives, which, he contended, effectively controlled major domestic political and social decision making. The strength of Mills's power elite rests on command and control, in which hierarchical structures are distinct and bureaucrats wield executive power (see also Domhoff 1967).

However, contemporary influence elites have moved away from these structural positions. Hierarchies co-exist with forms of power grounded in networks. Network-based power derives from players' positions in informal social networks and links to organisations and venues that, much more than in the past, connect elites across a global plane. Elites serve as connectors (see Savage and Williams 2008; Wedel 2009).

What created the space that this new breed of elites now controls? In short, the sea change—an unprecedented confluence of transformational developments over the past few decades: financialisation, which multiplies lucrative intermediary positions in finance while at the same time weakening the role of managerial elites; the privatisation, deregulation and governmental 'reform' fervour that began to take hold in the United States and the United Kingdom in the early 1980s; the Cold War's end a decade later, dispersing global authority and opening up sparsely governed arenas; and the rise of the Internet soon after (see Wedel 2009, 2014; Davis and Williams, forthcoming).

These developments have reconfigured the organisational ecosystem. They have created opportunities for all manner of players—from transnational networks laundering money or promoting human rights to consultants doing work previously performed by government employees and international organisations. In the United States, three-quarters of the people working for the federal government are employed through private companies, sometimes with a lot of influence and often with little oversight. Contractors run intelligence operations, control crucial databases, screen airport security and law-enforcement officials, choose and oversee other contractors and draft official documents (see Wedel 2009). The developments have spawned vehicles of influence that are set up or mobilized by elites: consulting, think tank, nongovernmental, and 'grassroots' organisations, ad hoc advisory groups and PR/lobbying firms. The sway of elites substantially resides in social networks that operate in and around these entities and venues. Thus, in contrast to C. Wright Mills's idea of *institutions* as pillars of power, today *influence elites* themselves can be seen as pillars of power.

A look at elite practices today provides a window into why traditional, still-dominant frameworks fall short. The four characteristics outlined ahead suggest ways to revise our understanding of how influence works in modern democracies.

A Novel Modus Operandi

First, influence elites often operate off the grid. On the world stage, crucial policies ranging from finance to media to technology are framed, sometimes even forged, outside the bureaucracies of governments, international organisations and companies. A case in point is the Group of Thirty (G-30), the Consultative Group on International Economic and Monetary Affairs. Its member list is a Who's Who of global economic policy influencers, including many Americans. Eleni Tsingou, who studied the group, describes it as 'part think tank, part interest group, and part club' (Seabrooke and Tsingou 2009, 20) formed of 'actors who write the rules' (Tsingou 2012, 4, 249). Its executive director told me, 'We don't make policy . . . but you can see our recommendations ending up in policy' (Wedel 2014, 20–23). One example of this is the hugely consequential issue of derivatives trading. In the 1990s, big banks didn't welcome increased regulation over their fast-emerging profit centres. Here, the G-30's study group and report on derivatives in the early 1990s, run by senior investment bankers such as then J. P. Morgan's CEO Dennis Weatherstone, helped solidify the standards for 'best practices.' This laissez-faire approach, made informally and then enshrined as policy, allowed derivatives to lay dynamite throughout the global financial system.

With regard to individual influence elites, much lobbying in the United States has gone underground as well. Although registered lobbyists and interest groups remain powerful, they are joined by less visible power brokers—I call them *shadow lobbyists*—who choose not to register as lobbyists (see Wedel 2014). Where once a former high official might have sought the title of *lobbyist* to display influence, today he may choose to call himself a *strategist, adviser* or *government affairs specialist* and not register at all. The business of influencing has changed so much that the main trade association for lobbyists, the American League of Lobbyists, decided in 2013 to adopt a more innocuous name: *Association of Government Relations Professionals.* The number of registered lobbyists declined by nearly 23 percent from 2007 to 2015 (OpenSecrets.org 2016)—but who would argue that this means a decline in lobbying per se as unregistered shadow lobbyists take their place?

The second characteristic of modern influencing is that players perform a plethora of professional roles, some of which overlap, and it's difficult to tell where one ends and another begins. Players assume more roles, in more venues of influence, with more flexibility and movement and within a far shorter time frame than their predecessors.

Take, for instance, retired generals and admirals. As recently as twenty years ago, the majority of them retired to, say, play golf. Now, when these powerful men (and the occasional woman) retire, the majority remain in the defense arena. They embark on sprawling, post-military careers that mix advisory roles with private sector work (Bender 2010). Such trajectories were highlighted by a *New York Times* account of General Barry McCaffrey's career entitled 'One Man's Military-Industrial-Media Complex' (Barstow 2008).

Generals like McCaffrey often consult with defense companies or even set up their own (eponymous) firms. At the same time, a retired general might serve on government advisory boards, shaping policy or procurement directions. In the process, he likely gains access to proprietary information. He can then employ information he gleans from his advisory board roles to benefit his defense clients. The general can plausibly deny that the advice he offers his clients is related to the information and access he garners in his government role, and we, the public, have little means of knowing what is actually the case. Further, some retired generals and admirals add a think tank or university affiliation to their resume, building an image of gravitas and incorruptibility. And some include media commentator appearances, in which they are nearly always identified as retired generals, not as in their more current and lucrative consultancy roles.

Clearly, the system has moved beyond the proverbial 'revolving door'. That model has only one exit point: The regulator or congressman joins a lobbying firm. The revolving door now features multiple entry and exit points. A player exits to a business, think tank, consultancy firm, university or media outlet and straddles two or more roles at the same time. Although the conventional revolving door player passing from point A to B and back again remains an important staple, his avant-garde counterpart is more elusive. He may wield more influence—and is less accountable.

Vehicles of Influence

Think tanks, consulting firms, non-profits, and grassroots organisations have proliferated in recent years. Many are empowered or even established by influence elites to sway policy and public opinion. Thus, a third characteristic of today's influence elites is that they create their own organisational vehicles. Although they help shape important policy decisions, they are not registered lobbyists, interest groups or other conventional influencers.

Think Tank-Corporate/Billionaire-Government-Media Complex

Think tanks lend an impartial, scholarly imprimatur, through which influence can be laundered. By at least one estimate, the United States has upwards of 1,830 such organisations today, a figure that's more than doubled since 1980 (McGann 2015, 10, 54) and actually may be far higher (Bender 2013).

Neither think tanks nor think tanks with ideological bents are new. Yet although they have traditionally conducted serious, even multiyear studies, today many have become partisan fighters, armed with media-friendly reports and minute-to-minute messaging. They prize 'impact' and metrics to show donors, sometimes sole benefactors. They are often populated by former journalists. Their stars create buzz on social media and TV and organize invitation-only conferences of power brokers. The time horizon of this new-style outfit is shorter than its older-style counterpart; many have only been around for only a few years. A new species has been born that, though it might still be called a think tank, is enmeshed in a new ecosystem (McGann 2015).

With a scholarly veneer and journalists at the ready, think tanks are perfect vehicles through which influence elites can drive consensus in a certain direction. Take, for instance, the COINdinistas (*COIN* stands for *counterinsurgency*) and their influence on the conduct of US wars in Afghanistan and Iraq. To pursue their strategy of engagement with local populations to counteract insurgencies, a collection of generals (including David Petraeus), influential military reporters, scholars, defense contractors and policy makers coalesced around COIN. At times, they circumvented the bureaucracy, using as their vehicle of influence a new Washington think tank, the Center for a New American Security (CNAS), which was substantially funded by defense companies. With CNAS as a mouthpiece and site of power, the COINdinistas played a key role in making and justifying the military policy for recent years of the Afghanistan war. Deploying CNAS-affiliated reporters across the media, they swayed public and policymaker opinion to their side. By effectively sidelining the bureaucracy and enlisting the media to help, they won the fight and left their colleagues with little choice but to walk with them.

Consulting-Corporate-Government Complex

In the past, consulting firms engaged primarily in private sector work. Today, they sometimes stand in for government to perform core government functions, often with little or no oversight from actual government employees. Contractors run intelligence operations, control crucial databases, choose and oversee other contractors and draft official documents (Wedel 2010).

Ambiguity is an important quality that grants deniability to consulting firms that perform government work—or serve as an interface between government and companies. Take, for instance, Promontory Financial Group. Shrouded in ambiguity, Promontory performs multiple, potentially overlapping roles. An *American Banker* profile used these phrases to describe Promontory: 'sort of ex-regulator omnibus'; 'shadow network between banks and regulators'; and 'an auxiliary . . . private-sector regulator'. Or, even more category-defying: 'a kind of arbitrage and interlocution between regulators and banks' (see Horwitz and Aspan 2013).

With nineteen offices from Toronto to Tokyo, Washington, DC, and beyond, Promontory has served as a private consultant to Bank of America, Morgan Stanley, Wells Fargo, PNC, Allied Irish, and the Vatican bank. Promontory is hired for crisis management or to navigate new regulations meant to rein in some of the banks' forays into exotic derivatives and proprietary trading. Almost two-thirds of Promontory's approximately 170 senior executives have been employed by regulatory agencies (see Protess and Silver-Greenberg 2013).

One of Promontory's potentially overlapping roles is that of ersatz regulator. The US government has dispersed and diluted its own authority by enlisting Promontory and similar firms. The most common variant of this, an informal one, appears to be that when banks hire Promontory, that act carries informal weight, which they can use to suggest that they are in compliance. In another variant, the formal outsourcing of authority, sometimes from the government itself, mandates that banks use Promontory or a similar firm to perform financial oversight, which in the past the government handled itself (Douglas 2013).

Among Promontory's other roles is that of 'shadow [unregistered] lobbyist' on behalf of its banker clients. With very recent government experience with regulations under consideration (by virtue of its ex-regulator employees), the firm has worked to defang the implementation of the Dodd-Frank legislation passed after the 2008 financial crisis and (shadow-)lobbied former regulatory colleagues to do so (Calabrese 2013). When the Dodd-Frank legislation eventually passed in 2010, after Wall Street poured huge amounts of money into blocking financial reform, the new game became impeding its implementation using the dense fine print of Dodd-Frank to achieve this.

In addition to shadow lobbying on behalf of specific clients, Promontory weighed in on the Volcker Rule, which holds that banks should be barred from investing depositors' dollars for institutional profit. This was part of the Dodd-Frank legislation, designed to rein in risky trading by US banks. Evidence indicates that Promontory was indeed at least somewhat involved when financial firms and regulators were hashing over the much-disputed rule (Calabresi 2013). Moreover, the *New York Times*, while analysing data from a non-profit that studied the issue, found in 2013 that although Promontory hadn't been a registered lobbyist for four years, 'the firm's executives have met with regulators at least 10 times in the last two years on thorny issues like the . . . Volcker Rule' (Protess and Silver-Greenberg 2013). Of course, Promontory insisted to the *New York Times* that meetings do not necessarily constitute 'lobbying'.

Promontory exemplifies entangled allegiances and shifting roles as the firm bends with the whims of its clients (at times even standing in for regulators as overseers and auditors). It has served as a sort of proxy for government auditors, paid by those it audits. The firm also acts as an unconventional lobbying outfit, intervening with regulators on behalf of its clients and buffering clients from regulation through shadow lobbying.

The issues highlighted by Promontory are emblematic of new-style entities used by influence elites. It is not a registered lobbyist, accounting firm, or government regulator. With no fixed identity, it can flex to suit the occasion. The enigma that is Promontory serves its own and its clients' purposes well; but can the same be said for public accountability?

Grassroots (or Non-profit)-Corporate/Billionaire-Media Complex

Many 'grassroots' and non-profit entities are equally steeped in ambiguity and lack accountability. Some campaign fund-raising groups pose as non-profits or grassroots organisations, promoting the cause of an unseen backer in ways that make it appear to be a grassroots movement (Wedel 2014). The phrase *dark money* conjures up untraceable campaign financing, but elections aren't the only way to influence policy. Donors and corporate interests fund purported grassroots organisations or non-profits, which lend the veneer of civic action, often in nearly untraceable ways. These entities range from 'patient advocacy' groups funded by pharmaceutical companies to 'safe energy' organisations supported by the nuclear industry. What in common parlance are called *front groups* and *astroturfing* are not new, but the digital age has made it infinitely easier to mimic a grassroots campaign for a wide audience.

The advent of the Internet and social media, as well as the near gutting of investigative journalism, have also nurtured simulacra—things that *look* or *feel like* the real thing but aren't. Big donors and corporations are creating the simulacrum of a real, organically created movement that just happens to serve their interests. For example, the Facebook page of the Koch Industries-supported group Americans for Prosperity boasts a more than one-million-strong 'standing army' of anti-tax activists, but no mention of its billionaire sponsors.

The giveaway signposts include the following:

• Innocuous-sounding names, evoking citizens' advocacy or genuine do-it-yourself efforts

• Organisations and efforts staged from the top—be they by a handful of billionaires or a cadre around a charismatic leader (for example, Barack Obama's 501c4 group Organizing for Action)

• Entities that morph their purposes in ways convenient for their unseen sponsors

• Organisations to create an echo chamber and make it appear that there's a larger movement than there actually is

• The use of big names or former top officials to give organisations heft

• Sponsorship and funding sources that are indirect and almost impossible to track

In short, these are enterprises with influence steeped in obscurity, lending themselves deniability.

Although these new-style think tanks, consulting firms, non-profits and grassroots organisations are not typically included in the framework of political influence, they should be. They have become a crucial part of the repertoire of influence elites.

The Clinton Playbook

These novel means of wielding influence—and more—are on full display when it comes to high-profile elites such as former US President Bill Clinton (former British Prime Minister Tony Blair exhibits a similar pattern). Clinton's player status has called into question policy decisions made by Hillary Clinton while she was secretary of state and guaranteed further questions. Bill Clinton's playbook consists of several boundary-blurring strategies employed together.

Clinton employs two strategies that I've already introduced in spades: crafting overlapping roles and creating entities of influence. He established the sprawling Clinton Foundation and its non-profit Global Initiative while serving as a paid adviser to a private equity/consulting firm called Teneo (among other business ventures). Teneo co-founder Douglas Band reportedly recruited donors to be Teneo clients and vice versa.

Not only has Clinton set up vehicles of influence, but the criss-crossing entities are tailor-made for deniability, one (or sometimes two or three) steps removed from themselves. This former statesman enlists friends and allies. When donations come even one step removed, the recipient can distance himself when it's expedient to do so. The Clinton Global Initiative, for instance, advises companies on philanthropy instead of doling out the money itself, providing distance should questions arise over possible conflicts of interest. When the entities are subject to different laws, even more deniability is possible. We saw that in spring 2015, when reports surfaced of more than a thousand undisclosed donors to a Clinton-affiliated charity in Canada that aimed to sign uranium-mining deals needing approval from Hillary Clinton's State Department. The Clinton Foundation could conveniently argue that Canadian law protects donors' anonymity to charities.

Another playbook strategy is celebrity branding. The Clinton Global Initiative's annual meeting skilfully employs the lure of celebrity-hood. It has a five-figure entrance fee that brings the powerful together to network and hash out global issues, in the style of the annual Davos meeting. The *New Republic* has described it thusly: 'For corporations, attaching Clinton's brand to their social investments offered a major PR boost . . . There's an undertow of transactionalism in the glittering annual dinners . . . the fixation on celebrity, and a certain contingent of donors whose charitable contributions and business interests occupy an uncomfortable proximity' (MacGillis 2013).

Clearly, conventional notions of political influence cannot begin to chart the flexibility of roles and criss-crossing entities of today's top players and the deniability these afford, the role of branding and celebrity status in their success and the players' potential impact beyond accountability.

Power Cliques

That impact beyond accountability is magnified when influence elites work together in social networks toward mutual agendas.

Today's influence elites often form tight-knit, trust-based, enduring networks.

I have chronicled the organisation and effect of several of these power cliques, including the Wall Street-Washington circle that has had a huge impact on the global economy through its decisions about the regulation of exotic derivatives trading (see Wedel 2014); the 'Neocon core', the members of which had been working together in various incarnations for several decades and helped take the United States to war in Iraq in 2003 (Wedel 2009); and the COINdinistas discussed earlier.

What I call *flex nets* are the ultimate power cliques. Flex nets are trust-based groups powered by shared ideology and noted for their members' loyalty. They coordinate influence from multiple moving perches, inside and outside official structures. They thwart both bureaucratic and professional authority by creating network-based structures and personalized practices within government while circumventing standard ones and marginalizing officials who are not part of their network. They relax both governments' rules of accountability and businesses' codes of competition, thereby challenging principles that have defined both modern democratic states and free markets (Wedel 2009, 15–21).

Flex nets are a paradox in terms of political influence: more amorphous and less transparent than conventional political lobbies and interest groups, yet also more coherent and less accountable. Thus, while administrations come and go, flex nets persist. They are not the instruments of any particular administration, even when their members occupy official positions within it. As members spin overlapping roles at the nexus of official and private power, they create a virtually closed loop that challenges accountability—often far removed from public input, knowledge or potential sanction.

Today, many conditions that facilitated Mills's power elite—stable positions at the top of enduring institutions exerting command and control—no longer prevail. These hierarchies have not vanished, but they have transmuted amid the transformational developments here outlined. Flexible, mobile and multi-positioned, influence elites serve as connectors, intermeshing hierarchies and networks in complex ways. In contrast to the greater and more predictable role of hierarchies in Mills's day, some levers of influence have moved several steps away, rendering public input and accountability more inscrutable. The way influence elites are organized and the modus operandi they employ to wield influence enable them to evade public accountability, a hallmark of democratic society.

Today's influence elites and the vehicles they use to help organize sway do not fit conventional notions of political influence. Clearly, we need to update our understanding.

References

Barstow, D. 2008. "One Man's Military-Industrial-Media Complex." *New York Times*, November 29. http://www.nytimes.com/2008/11/30/washington/30general.html?pagewanted=all.

Bender, B. 2010. "From the Pentagon to the Private Sector." *Boston Globe*, December 26. http://www.boston.com/news/nation/washington/articles/2010/12/26/defense_firms_lure_retired_generals/.

Bender, B. 2013. "Many D.C. Think Tanks Now Players in Partisan Wars." *Boston Globe*, August 11. https://www.bostonglobe.com/news/nation/2013/08/10/brain-trust-for-sale-the-growing-footprint-washington-think-tank-industrial-complex/7ZifHfrLPlbz0bSeVOZHdI/story.html.

Calabresi, M. 2013. "Promontory's Role in the Dodd-Frank Game." *Time*, September 16. http://swampland.time.com/2013/09/16/ one-firms-role-in-the-dodd-frank-game/.

Davis, A., and K. Williams. Forthcoming. "Introduction to Elites and Power after Financialization." *Theory, Culture and Society*.

Domhoff, G. 1967. *William, Who Rules America?* Englewood Cliffs, NJ: Prentice-Hall.

Douglas, D. 2013. "The Rise of Promontory." *Washington Post*, August 2. http:// www.washingtonpost.com/business/economy/the-rise-ofpromontory/ 2013/08/02/c187a112-f32b-11e2-bdae-0d1f78989e8a_story.html.

Horwitz, J., and M. Aspan. 2013. "How Promontory Financial Became Banking's Shadow Regulator." *American Banker*, March 15. http://www .americanbanker.com/magazine/123_4/how-promontory-financial -becamebanking-s-shadow-regulator-1057480-1.html.

MacGillis, A. 2013. "Scandal at Clinton Inc.: How Doug Brand Drove a Wedge through a Political Dynasty." *Salon*, September 22. http://www.newrepublic .com/article/114790/how-doug-band-drove-wedge-through-clinton-dynasty.

McGann, J. 2015. "2014 Global Go-To Think Tank Index." Think Tank and Civil Societies Program, University of Pennsylvania. http://repository.upenn.edu/ cgi/viewcontent.cgi?article=1008&context=think_tanks.

Mills, C. Wright. 1956. *The Power Elite*. New York: Oxford University Press.

OpenSecrets.org. 2016. "Lobbying Database." Center for Responsive Politics. https://www.opensecrets.org/lobby/.

Protess, B., and J. Silver-Greenberg. 2013. "Former Regulators Find a Home with a Powerful Firm." *New York Times*, April 9. http://dealbook.nytimes .com/2013/04/09/for-former-regulators-a-home-on-wall-street/.

Savage, M., and K. Williams. 2008. *Remembering Elites*. Oxford: Wiley-Blackwell.

Seabrooke, L., and E. Tsingou. 2009. "Revolving Doors and Linked Ecologies in the World Economy: The Practice of International Financial Reform." CSGR Working Paper no. 260/09, Centre for the Study of Globalisation and Regionalisation, University of Warwick. https://www2.warwick.ac.uk/fac/soc/ pais/research/researchcentres/csgr/papers/260-09.pdf.

Tsingou, E. 2012. "Club Model Politics and global Financial Governance: The Case of the Group of Thirty." Ph.D diss., FMG: Amsterdam Institute for Social Science Research (AISSR). http://dare.uva.nl/document/2/145922.

Wedel, J. R. 2009. *Shadow Elite: How the World's New Power Brokers Undermine Democracy, Government, and the Free Market*. New York: Basic Books.

Wedel, J. R. 2010. "Selling Out Uncle Sam: How the Myth of Small Government Undermines National Security." New America Foundation, August. http://www.newamerica.net/sites/newamerica.net/files/policydocs/SellingOut UncleSamAug10.pdf.

Wedel, J. R. 2014. *Unaccountable: How the Establishment Corrupted Our Finances, Freedom and Politics and Created an Outsider Class*. New York: Pegasus Books.

17

'Public Knowledge' and Health Policy

Colin Leys

Aeron Davis's succinct overview of the contemporary determinants of the quality of public knowledge provides many of
the elements needed for understanding what has happened to
public knowledge about health policy since 1980. But knowledge about health care is not merely subject to the general impact of global market forces outlined by Davis in chapter 1, and
the increased complexity of modern knowledge. Being almost
entirely state-funded in Britain, and therefore a prime object of
state policy, health care is also subject to a critical shift that has
simultaneously taken place in the way all policy is made. The
end of the hegemony of social democracy in the United Kingdom in the late 1970s saw the end of the liberal/social-demo-
cratic 'policy regime' that had been in place since the 1920s, if
not earlier.[1] The neoliberal policy regime that has replaced it
effectively rejects—in intention and increasingly in practice—
the concept of a 'public sphere' to which the concept of public

knowledge is necessarily linked, and this is nowhere more evident than in relation to health policy.

The Institutional Foundations of the Public Sphere

The public sphere was above all a construct of the institutions through which social, economic and political knowledge was produced and assessed and policies were endorsed, independently of the influence of private interests. These institutions were the professions, insulated from both commercial pressures and from government; the universities, funded through arms-length arrangements to preserve their freedom to engage in disinterested teaching and research; the press, with freedom to allow for the exposure of official dissimulation or lies; public service broadcasting, to give the electorate valid information and a platform for public debate on how the information should be interpreted; judges, funded from the civil list to make them able to stand up to governments; and the senior civil service, dedicated to ensuring that policy was made in light of the public knowledge made possible by these arrangements.

The idea of a public sphere was thus closely linked to the idea of the public interest. At a minimum, the concept of the public interest is something distinct from, or which transcends, private interests, and involves a commitment to a norm of disinterestedness; but it could also connote substantive values, such as that human happiness should be maximised, for example, or that everyone should be as healthy as possible. As soon as this is acknowledged it is obvious that the idea that public knowledge as something universally shared is inherently problematic. At any given time, there is typically a body of conventional wisdom, the dominant ideas and norms of the day, that can be described as *shared*. But this set of ideas and norms is always contested. In the case of health, we are witnessing a drive to devalue and if possible eliminate a former body of 'common sense' and replace it with one according to which, instead of policy being produced in the public sphere to serve the public interest, it should be produced by whatever means will simply make markets efficient. Rupert Murdoch's statement in relation to broadcasting that 'the public interest is what interests the public' was a fair representation of the neoliberal viewpoint; that is, the elite who have occupied the key roles in the public sphere are unrepresentative, and their claim to uphold an interest shared by everyone is undemocratic and invalid. On this view the only valid ground for any statement about interests is consumer preferences.

Dismantling the Public Sphere in Health Policy

From the early 1980s onwards the NHS became a priority target for neoliberals of this kind for several reasons. First, accounting as it did for about 15 percent of state expenditure, it was seen as a potentially major field for private capital accumulation. Second, being tax-funded and equally accessible to all, it was a bastion of social-democratic values and a constant reminder of the advantages and popularity of non-commodified services. Moreover, because there is a steep class gradient in ill-health, spending on health care necessarily also involves some income redistribution from rich to poor, not just from the well to the ill. For all these reasons, the NHS was one of the first branches of the state to feel the effects of the new neoliberal policy regime, beginning with a radical reorganisation of the Department of Health (DH).

The erosion of the department's policy-making function has been the most complete of any government department. Since the creation of the NHS Executive in 1989, which shifted effective power over policy more and more into the hands of health service managers, the DH has been steadily run down, declining from 4,795 staff in 1996 (UK Government 2015) to 2,422 in 2013, of whom only 164 were in the senior civil service (a further cull of 650 DH posts was announced in February 2016; see BBC 2016), and almost all of these had been recruited from hospital management or, increasingly, from private sector sources, especially management consultancies. Of the thirty-two members of the 'top' team in 2006, eighteen were drawn from NHS management and six from the private sector; only one was a career civil servant (Greer and Jarman 2007, table 1). From 2003 to 2010, a 180-strong Commercial Directorate, consisting almost entirely of 'interims' seconded from the private sector, infused the DH with a market-oriented culture, while senior DH personnel moved in the opposite direction into senior jobs with private health companies, as did several former Labour ministers following the 2010 election.[2]

In this way, the defence of the public interest in health policy that was formerly provided by the senior civil service's role in policy-making was effectively abolished; instead, from 2000 to 2010, the development of health policy was in practice largely outsourced to a mixture of management consultancies and two well-funded think tanks, the Kings Fund and the Nuffield Trust, the latter of which had strong ties with the private sector. McKinsey & Co. in particular played a major role in Labour's health policy thinking in those years and is credited with shaping much of the detail of the coalition government's 2012 Health and Social Care Act.

A further effect of the market-creation drive was to reduce the amount of information on the basis of which policy can be evaluated. For example, details of how the £60 billion plus a year now channelled through Clinical Commissioning Groups (CCGs) to pay the providers of secondary care is spent are no longer centrally collected. Moreover, most CCGs have outsourced the making and management of the contracts for these services to Commissioning Support Units (CSUs), embryonic management companies formed by the remaining staff of the now disbanded Primary Care Trusts, with the effect that many details of the expenditure of even a single CCG are not obtainable by public researchers (CHPI 2015). The combination of these factors means that the information needed for the critical evaluation of the outsourcing of acute hospital and community care scarcely exists.

These developments in health policy took place in the context of another general development in the erosion of the public sphere: the normalisation of spin (see Cave and Rowell 2014, chap. 4). The rapid development of new techniques for influencing public opinion coincided with the arrival in office in 1997 of a Labour leadership determined not to allow the right-wing press to repeat the savaging that had been meted out to the party between 1981 and 1992. In office, the party invested heavily in media management. Government publications became like corporate publications, designed to convey positive feelings and downplay bad news. Lord Darzi's 2008 report on healthcare for England, to which McKinsey & Co. staff also made a large input, was a prime example of this style (Department of Health 2008). Another was McKinsey & Co.'s 2009 report on 'Achieving World Class Productivity' (McKinsey & Co. 2009). This report, in the form of PowerPoint slides, called for a programme of 'efficiency savings' based on manifestly unrealistic assumptions and financial projections for which no accessible sources were provided. Yet it became the basis of policy, whereby NHS managers were called on to maintain or even improve services while losing £20 billion in funding over five years. By 2010, no one seriously concerned with health policy any longer placed great confidence in the value of statements or claims emanating from the DH.[3]

As for the production of public knowledge by the fourth estate, the negative pressures itemised by Aeron Davis apply in spades to health policy. Health policy is complex and undramatic—and unattractive to editors at a time when newspapers are desperate to stem the loss of readers while simultaneously cutting editorial staff and making those who remain work longer and across more media. The temptation to rely on government press releases is nowhere stronger than in health policy.

On top of these general pressures there is the threat to public service broadcasting represented by the demand from private broadcasters for a slice of the television licence fee. Following the brutalisation of the BBC by Alastair Campbell for exposing the Blair government's duplicity over the 'dodgy dossier' on Iraq, successive Directors General and BBC trustees seem to have concluded that the corporation's future depends on recognising that the midpoint of the party political spectrum had moved decisively to the right. How far the BBC's startlingly uncritical treatment of the 2011 Health and Social Care Bill was conscious policy, as opposed to the more or less unconscious internalisation of the new ideological reality by senior BBC staff, it is impossible to say. As Oliver Huitson notes in his review (Huitson 2013) of the failure of the media to provide a critical understanding of the Bill, the real aim of the legislation was too obvious to be overlooked, and a very large gap opened up between the mainstream discourse on health policy and that of the social media. This raises interesting questions: In the era of globalised capitalism, how far does the operation of representative government need shared public knowledge? Do voters increasingly expect to be told nothing they can really trust? How far does voters' resulting indifference pose a significant threat to the legitimacy of the government and the representative state?

Two other notional pillars of the public sphere have proved fatally weak in relation to health policy: (1) the medical profession and (2) academic experts. Margaret Thatcher's view that the professions were market-constraining monopolies that needed to be brought to heel led to a new culture of criticism of doctors and to considerable inroads into their independence and prestige. In 1945–1946, the BMA had come close to refusing to operate the new health service; in 1987 the presidents of the three biggest Royal Colleges of medicine took the opposite stand, this time in defence of the NHS, writing a joint open letter to the Prime Minister to protest the financial strangulation to which the NHS was being subjected. By 2010–2012, such confident behaviour was no longer thinkable. The BMA and the Academy of Royal Colleges were in a position to make it politically impossible for the Coalition to push through the HSC Bill, and over the months from July 2010 (when the white paper outlining the Bill was published) to the Bill's passage into law in 2012, a majority of doctors became more and more opposed to it. But their leaders refused to adopt a position of categorical opposition or to actively communicate their members' views to the public. Among many possible explanations, the most likely, as well as the most charitable, is that the leaders were ultimately more committed to the interests of the profession than to those of the public and judged that they could not afford to lose government patronage (see Davis and Wrigley 2013).

As for health policy academics, there too there is now an alignment of interest towards government policy rather than to the public interest. The conversion of universities into institutions primarily concerned with producing trained manpower for corporations and research useful for making money has been underpinned by their reconfiguration as businesses (McGettigan 2013). Research funding from the Economic and Social Research Council is explicitly oriented to the promotion of economic competitiveness, and much academic work on health policy is directly financed by the DH.[4] There is strong pressure from university administrators to secure research grants, and there are few charitable funding sources that are not themselves aligned with government policy. In this context, few academics working on health policy, even among senior tenured staff, have been willing to become outspoken critics of the market-based model, even though both theory and empirical research show that market-based provision leads to higher costs and lower quality in health care. The pages of health policy journals contain much critical analysis of particular health policies, but it is mainly 'immanent' criticism relative to the expressed aims of policy, rather than critique based on any alternative conception of how the public interest might be served.

Conclusion

In conclusion, rather than seeing the issue in terms of the existence or non-existence of shared public knowledge, I am inclined to see it more in terms of competing visions of the public interest and competing knowledge paradigms derived from these visions, and to question how much the 'sufficient legitimacy' of election-based governments now depends on the paradigm favoured by the government of the day being widely shared. What is clear, though, is that in health policy the conditions for the maintenance of a concept of the public interest independent of politically dominant private interests have been largely destroyed, and with them the possibility of any coherent public discussion of health policy.

To take just one of many possible examples, consider the issue of cost, which is currently at the top of the political agenda. The question asked is whether the NHS is 'affordable'—but affordable by whom, and with reference to what standard of reasonableness?[5] In relation to the government's austerity spending plans? Or to the proportion of GDP spent on health, which remains substantially lower than in comparable countries?[6] How valid are the assumptions underpinning the claim that the NHS faces a £30 billion financial shortfall by 2021? What portion of this predicted shortfall is accounted for by the administrative and legal costs of operating the service as a market, compared with those of non-market provisions? What evidence is there that the costs of opening the NHS up to competition from private providers have been offset by increased efficiency? Is the problem primarily one of the scale of the resources needed, as opposed to a problem of resistance by corporations and wealthier taxpayers to raising the needed resources from taxation? Given the stakes, these are not unreasonable questions, but even if there was a shared willingness to seek objective answers to them—which there clearly is not— neither the data required nor adequate resources to study them any longer exist.

Notes

1. This is outlined in my essay 'The Cynical State' (Leys 2006).
2. The revolving door in health policy is discussed in Leys and Player (2011, 90–95), and the revolving door as a mechanism for the abolition of the civil service as a bastion of the public sphere generally is discussed in Leys (2012).
3. On official mendacity about health policy between 2003 and 2010, see Leys and Player 2011, chap. 8.
4. In 2012–2013, the DH spent almost £240 million on policy research; see Department of Health (2012–2013), paras 2.38–2.39.
5. In July 2016 the House of Lords established a committee to enquire into 'the long term sustainability of the NHS'. Its report was expected in March 2017.
6. See the Barker report (Barker 2014, 22), which pointed out that with very limited increases in spending on the NHS, 'by 2025 England's public spending on health and social care combined would barely match what comparable countries spent 15 years earlier.'

References

Barker, K. 2014. "A New Settlement for Health and Social Care." Commission on the Future of Health and Social Car in England. http://www.kingsfund.org.uk/sites/files/kf/field/field_publication_file/Commission%20Final%20%20interactive.pdf.

BBC. 2016. "Department of Health to Cut 650 Jobs to Reduce Costs." BBC, February 5. http://www.bbc.co.uk/news/health-35499277.

Cave, T., and A. Rowell. 2014. *A Quiet Word: Lobbying, Crony Capitalism and Broken Politics in Britain.* London: Bodley Head.

Centre for Health and the Public Interest (CHPI). 2015. "The Contracting NHS: Can the NHS Handle the Outsourcing of Clinical Services?" Centre for Health and the Public Interest, March. http://chpi.org.uk/wp-content/uploads/2015/04/CHPI-ContractingNHS-Mar-final.pdf.

Davis, J., and D. Wrigley. 2013. "The Silence of the Lambs." In *NHS SOS: How the NHS Was Betrayed—and How We Can Save It*, edited by J. Davis and R. Tallis, 62–87. London: Oneworld.

Department of Health. 2008. "High Quality Care for All: NHS Next Stage Review Final Report."

Department of Health. 2012–2013. "Annual Report and Accounts 2012–13."

Greer, S., and H. Jarman. 2007. *The Department of Health and the Civil Service: From Whitehall to Department of Delivery to Where?* London: Nuffield Trust.

Huitson, O. 2013. "Hidden in Plain Sight." In *NHS SOS: How the NHS Was Betrayed—and How We Can Save It*, edited by J. Davis and R. Tallis, 150–173. London: Oneworld.

Leys, C. 2006. "The Cynical State." In *Telling the Truth: Socialist Register*, edited by L. Panitch and C. Leys, 1–27. London: Merlin Press.

Leys, C. 2012. "The Dissolution of the Mandarins: The Sell-Off of the British State." openDemocracy UK, June 15. https://www.opendemocracy.net/ourkingdom/colin-leys/dissolution-of-mandarins-sell-off-of-british-state.

Leys, C., and S. Player. 2011. *The Plot against the NHS*. London: Merlin Press.

McGettigan, A. 2013. *The Great University Gamble*. London: Pluto Press.

McKinsey & Co. 2009. "Achieving World Class Productivity in the NHS 2009/10–2013/14: Detailing the Size of the Opportunity." Department of Health, March. http://webarchive.nationalarchives.gov.uk/20130107105354/http://www.dh.gov.uk/prod_consum_dh/groups/dh_digitalassets/documents/digitalasset/dh_116521.pdf.

UK Government. 2015. https://www.gov.uk/government/uploads/system/uploads/attachment_data/file/390893/DH_WMI_Nov-14.csv/preview.

18

Conclusion:
Manifesto for Public Knowledge

Des Freedman and Justin Schlosberg

This book has comprehensively identified the ways in which the institutions that have traditionally delivered shared forms of public knowledge have been undermined. It has argued that neoliberal principles, austerity-related economics and heavily segmented online content provision have shrunk and distorted the spaces through which citizens have come to know each other and learn about the world: through spheres of communication and media, education, politics and public affairs. This has led to a situation in which we are less able to exercise oversight over the structures and processes that shape our societies and therefore less likely to be informed by and participate in matters of huge public interest.

Public knowledge is not simply the mirror image of private provision and is not reducible to the production and circulation of a range of commodities that the market may or may not support. Its main goal is not to sell user data to digital intermediaries or audience attention to advertisers. Instead, it refers to a sphere of information and culture that is predicated on the need to serve the public interest, precisely because wholly market-driven transactions are likely to favour the circulation of knowledge that privileges elite networks and private channels. Public knowledge is the property of all citizens whose needs ought to be met, irrespective of their purchasing power, geographical location or social background.

Public knowledge is therefore a classic 'public good': a phenomenon that is 'non-rivalrous' in the sense that one person's consumption does not limit anyone else's enjoyment and in that its social benefit is maximised the more people have access to it. Typical public goods, according to Onora O'Neill (2016, 174), include 'a sound currency, a non-corrupt judiciary, a medical database, a common language, flood controls systems, lighthouses and street lighting'—to which we might add an impartial news system, public service broadcasting, free and accessible higher education, a well-funded library service and non-proprietary digital networks that are free at the point of use.

We are concerned that public goods are being circumscribed by their for-profit counterparts. We want to help wrest control of knowledge-producing and decision-making back from structures that are not only largely unaccountable to their users but also explicitly intertwined with the powerful interests that need regulating in the first place.

We acknowledge both the scope and limits of participatory and networked forms of resistance that can and have engendered new communicative spaces in which public knowledge goods thrive—but they are constrained by repressive forces of audience segmentation, atomisation and surveillance, as well as enduring divides in media access and literacy. Progressive reforms must be oriented towards *publicising* these spaces through forms of regulation that promote privacy rights, meaningful diversity of exposure and genuine equality of access. At the same time, old bottlenecks and traditional forms of gatekeeping power persist. There is still a knowledge *agenda*— one which transcends fragmented and polarized social groups and one which the prevailing empirical evidence suggests is still dominated by a handful of institutional megaphones. In attempting to address and challenge both new and old forms of concentrated communicative power, we need to ask: *Who* are the megaphones? *How* do their voices come to be amplified? *What* is the extent of their influence over public knowledge and debate?

In order to achieve this, we will need to do three things: First, we will have to demystify prevailing narratives about the knowledge society and associated civic empowerment. The bulk of available empirical evidence suggests that we have not entered, and are not entering, a golden age in which information flows freely and in which citizens are the exclusive determinants of the forms of knowledge, information and culture that achieve salience in the public domain. We have not witnessed the democratisation of gatekeeping power once vested in the owners and managers of news organisations, universities, publishers, film studios, record companies, television networks and other incumbent producers of knowledge and culture.

Second, we need to pay heed to the emergence of new forms of gatekeeping power vested in digital monopolies that control the means by which we encounter and engage with information, public knowledge and culture. However, whilst the prevailing *critical* narrative of the knowledge society suggests that digital monopolies have supplanted the power of 'old media', this notion misses a crucial point: that behind the discursive struggles and legal battles between dominant producers and intermediaries is a reality of growing interconnectedness and mutual dependence. Content is the bread and butter of search and social media industries, whilst the network 'switch' that they control—connecting that content with users—has become the lifeline of the content industries.

Finally, we need to reject an overarching instrumentalist logic about the efficiency of markets and crude audits and put in its place a different logic: one that is based on the adoption of progressive principles that are aimed at securing the *conditions* in which public knowledge can be protected and nurtured. These conditions might include the following:

- *Independence:* The ability to be meaningfully autonomous of vested interests

- *Diversity:* The recognition of minority interests and groups and a commitment to articulate differences rather than to impose an artificial consensus

- *Universality:* The need to cater to all groups irrespective of geography, background and status and to challenge any attempts to exclude users on the basis of their inability to pay

- *Plurality:* The provision of multiple sources of public knowledge rather than monopolistic or oligopolistic control over knowledge markets

- *Redistribution:* The commitment to address structural barriers to participate in knowledge sectors and to highlight funding streams that better allocate funds on the basis of need and ability to pay

- *Transparency:* The requirement for public knowledge producers to declare any interests that may impede their ability to provide independent and trusted services

- *Accountability:* The ability for publics to scrutinize and influence the services carried out on their behalf

These principles could be realized in the following mechanisms and commitments:

- Ring-fence public funds to support the creation and dissemination of public knowledge and to nurture an education and knowledge infrastructure that can help grow the economy.

- Where production is carried out by private bodies, these organizations should make an explicit commitment to the maximization of human capital and public, rather than shareholder, value.

- Create provisions for broadband infrastructures that are designed and operated as public utilities rather than gated communities.

- Establish strong 'net neutrality' rules to ensure that online channels remain non-discriminatory and open to all.

- Protect privacy and the safeguarding of data. Just as there is a requirement in many cities for private developers to provide affordable housing in any new complex, digital intermediaries should be required to provide spaces that are entirely free of cookies and tracking devices that undermine the privacy of users and commodify their data.

- Use taxes and levies on the profits of private information intermediaries to support non-profit knowledge producers—for example, new forms of public interest journalism, public education, specialist legal support and digital content creation.

- Enhance the transparency of meetings and relations between senior media, public affairs and political figures, ensuring that details of interactions are published in a more timely, accessible and comprehensible manner.

Conclusion

A truly progressive reform agenda requires attention to both nurturing new vehicles of public knowledge production and delivery and to reconfiguring old ones in ways that make them more democratic, accountable and sustainable. In regard to the former, there is a particular pressing need to examine the effects on public knowledge caused by intensifying collaboration between dominant players in the supply of news and information. Tech giants have become the means by which some news brands are reaching greater audiences than ever before, but also the cause of enveloping market failure in the business of news. In the shadow of this interplay, particular vehicles for public knowledge goods are facing acute and in some cases existential pressures.

This is especially the case when it comes to developing local and long-form journalism outside of both state and market control. Regenerating these critical spheres of knowledge and cultural production will not provide a panacea to the problems discussed in this volume—but it does offer a starting point, because news is the principal means through which most people in advanced capitalist societies relate to and engage with civic life.

Beyond the news, institutions that have delivered public knowledge such as universities, libraries and public service broadcasting have rightly been criticized for being at times too elitist, too paternalistic, too cautious or too distant. In addition, these institutions have often been forced to compete with commercial providers or to discipline themselves to act more decisively as neoliberal subjects. What should be a wonderful idea—of an emancipatory and non-proprietary form of culture—has therefore been distorted by the pressures under which it is forced to operate. We want to secure opportunities for public knowledge that are truly independent of state and market and that facilitate instead a critical and expansive engagement with the world in which we live.

All of this requires extensive efforts in organization and translation so that the evolving constraints on public knowledge become more *visible* and ideas for progressive reforms more *audible* in both policy and public debate. There is a need to draw connections too with wider reform movements in the spheres of economic, environmental and social justice and in the struggle against the iniquities and injustices of global capitalism.

Reference

O'Neill, O. 2016. "Public Service Broadcasting, Public Value and Public Goods." In *A Future for Public Service Television: Content and Platforms in a Digital World*, 173–174. London: Goldsmiths, University of London. http://www .futureoftv.org.uk/report.

Contributors

Toril Aalberg is a professor at the Department of Sociology and Political Science at the Norwegian University of Science and Technology Trondheim. She is the author or editor of eight books, some in conjunction with others. These include *Challenges to Representative Democracy* (1999), *Achieving Justice* (2003), *Communicating Politics* (2007), *How Media Inform Democracy* (2012) and *Populist Political Communication in Europe* (2016).

Ian Anstice (ianlibrarian@live.co.uk) runs the Public Libraries News website (www.publiclibrariesnews.com), which is the main source of information on the sector and is used regularly by library staff, users, politicians and the media. He has been working as a professional librarian since 1994 and was recently made an honorary fellow of the Chartered Institute of Library and Information Professionals. He is currently a library manager in North West England.

Philip Augar is a former banker and the author of several books and many articles in the *Financial Times* and other publications. He is a visiting fellow at the Institute of Historical Research and has a doctorate in history.

Rodney Benson is a professor in the Department of Media, Culture, and Communication at New York University. He is the author of *Shaping Immigration News: A French-American Comparison* (2013), editor (with Erik Neveu) of *Bourdieu and the Journalistic Field* (2005) and co-author (with Matthew Powers) of *Public Media and Political Independence: Lessons for the Future of Journalism from Around the World* (2011).

Aeron Davis is a professor of political communication and co-director of PERC at Goldsmiths, University of London. His work crosses media sociology, political communications and economic sociology. He is the author of *Public Relations Democracy* (2002), *The Mediation of Power* (2007), *Political Communications and Social Theory* (2010) and *Promotional Cultures* (2013).

Des Freedman is a professor of media and communications at Goldsmiths, University of London. He is the author of *The Contradictions of Media Power* (2014) and *The Politics of Media Policy* (2008) and co-author (with James Curran and Natalie Fenton) of *Misunderstanding the Internet* (2016). He is the former chair of the Media Reform Coalition.

Wayne Hope is an associate professor in the School of Communication Studies, Auckland University of Technology. He co-edits the on-line journal *Political Economy of Communication*, and his most recent book is *Time, Communication and Global Capitalism* (2016).

Ken Jones is the senior policy officer at the National Union of Teachers. He was previously a professor of education at Goldsmiths, where he is now an emeritus professor. The second edition of his book *Education in Britain* was published in 2015.

Bong-hyun Lee has been a journalist in Korea since 1990. For most of his career, he has covered business issues. In 2012, he completed a doctorate in Goldsmiths' Media and Communications Department.

Colin Leys is an emeritus professor of political studies at Queen's University, Kingston, Canada, and an honorary research professor at Goldsmiths. His most recent books are *Market Driven Politics: Neoliberal Democracy and the Public Interest* (2001) and (with Stewart Player) *The Plot against the NHS* (2011). He is a member of the executive management team of the Centre for Health and the Public Interest (https://chpi.org.uk).

Andrew McGettigan lives in London and writes on higher education, philosophy and the arts. He is the author of *The Great University Gamble: Money, Markets and the Future of Higher Education* (2013). His writing has appeared in the *Guardian*, the *Observer*, *Times Higher Education*, *Research Fortnight*, *London Review of Books* and *Radical Philosophy*. He holds a doctorate in modern European philosophy. He blogs on higher education financing at https://andrewmcgettigan.org.

Michael Moran is professor of government at Alliance Business School, University of Manchester, and a member of CRESC. With the CRESC unit he has published a number of books, including *After the Great Complacence* (2011), *The End of the Experiment* (2014) and *What a Waste* (2015).

Aristotelis Nikolaidis (Aristotelis.Nikolaidis@brunel.ac.uk) has a PhD in media and communications from Goldsmiths, University of London. His work has been published in *Continuum: Journal of Media and Cultural Studies*, *Feminist Media Studies* and *Parliamentary Affairs*. He currently teaches at Brunel University and the University of Bedfordshire.

Justin Schlosberg is a lecturer in journalism and media in the Department of Film, Media and Cultural Studies at Birkbeck, University of London, and was network fellow at the Edmund

J. Safra Center for Ethics, Harvard University, in 2014–2015. He is the author of the forthcoming *Media Ownership and Agenda Control* (2016) and of *Power without Scrutiny: Media, Justice and Accountability* (2013). He is the current chair of the Media Reform Coalition.

Henry Silke is a lecturer in journalism in the School of Communication and Culture at the University of Limerick, Ireland. He has recently completed a PhD on the role of media and communications systems in capitalist crises. His other research interests include the political role of media and the potentialities of alternative media groups and movements. He writes and curates for Critical Media Review at https://criticalmediareview.wordpress.com/.

Roger Smith is a visiting professor at London South Bank University and has written extensively on legal aid and human rights. He is a solicitor who has been the director of JUSTICE and the Legal Action Group.

Peter A. Thompson (peter.thompson@vuw.ac.nz) is a senior lecturer in the media studies programme at Victoria University of Wellington. His main research interests concern media policy (especially funding mechanisms for public service media) and communication processes in financial markets. Peter is a founding editor of the *Political Economy of Communication* journal and currently is the vice-chair of the IAMCR Political Economy section.

Janine R. Wedel (jwedel@gmu.edu; on Twitter at @janinewedel), a social anthropologist, is a university professor in the School of Policy, Government, and International Affairs at George Mason University and currently also affiliated with the Hertie School in

Berlin. She is the author of *Unaccountable: How the Establishment Corrupted Our Finances, Freedom and Security and Created an Outsider Class* (2014) and the award-winning *Shadow Elite: How the World's New Power Brokers Undermine Democracy, Government, and the Free Market* (2009).

Karel Williams is professor at Alliance Business School and a director of CRESC, University of Manchester. With the CRESC unit he has published a number of books, including *After the Great Complacence* (2011), *The End of the Experiment* (2014) and *What a Waste* (2015).

Kate Wright is Chancellor's Fellow in the cultural and creative industries at the University of Edinburgh. Before moving to academia, she was an award-winning BBC journalist, in which role she spent nine years working on the Corporation's national and international flagship news programmes. She passed her PhD at Goldsmiths in February 2015.

Index